ALL OF US TOGETHER IN THE END

ALL OF US

TOGETHER

IN

THE END

MATTHEW VOLLMER

HUB CITY PRESS
SPARTANBURG, SC

Editor: Katherine Webb-Hehn
Cover and Book Design: Meg Reid
Cover Photograph © Sean Rayford
Author Photo © Todd Wemmer
Proofreader: Stephanie Trott

Library of Congress Cataloging-in-Publication Data

Vollmer, Matthew, author.
All of us together in the end / Matthew Vollmer.
Spartanburg, SC : Hub City Press, 2023.
LCCN 2022038936 (print) | LCCN 2022038937 (ebook)
ISBN   9798885740050 (trade paperback) | ISBN 9798885740067 (epub)
Subjects:
LCSH: Vollmer, Matthew—Family. | Authors, American—21st
   century—Family relationships. | Authors, American—21st
   century—Biography. | Vollmer, Matthew—Childhood and youth.
   Bereavement—Psychological aspects. | Memory—Psychological aspects.
   LCGFT: Autobiographies.
Classification:
LCC PS3622.O6435 Z46 2023 (print)
LCC PS3622.O6435 (ebook)
DDC 818/.603 [B]—dc23/eng/20221109

LC record available at https://lccn.loc.gov/2022038936
LC ebook record available at https://lccn.loc.gov/2022038937

Manufactured in the United States of America
First Edition

HUB CITY PRESS
200 Ezell Street
Spartanburg, SC 29306
864.577.9349 | www.hubcity.org

For my mother and father

(The scientist) Karl Popper was often heard to say, 'We don't know anything.' According to the British philosopher Brain McGee, he believed that this was the most important philosophical insight there is, which ought to inform all our philosophical activity. Human beings never achieve perfect knowledge, because anything we know at any given moment is invariably revised later. But far from being depressed by this, Popper found this constant engagement with insoluble problems an endless delight. One of the many great sources of happiness, he explained in his memoir, is to get a glimpse here and there of a new aspect of the incredible world we live in and of our incredible role in it.

Karen Armstrong, The Case for God

I thought you were an anchor in the drift of the world;
but no: there isn't an anchor anywhere.
There isn't an anchor in the drift of the world. Oh no.
I thought you were. Oh no. The drift of the world.

William Bronk, "The World"

I.   SOME WEIRD STUFF

On January 20, 2020, the first case of the coronavirus was detected in the United States. On this day, however, the word "coronavirus" was not trending on Twitter. Neither was "COVID-19." Or "quarantine." Or "pandemic." What terms were trending? "CurbYourEnthusiasm." And "Venus Williams" and "Warren and Klobuchar." And "Australian Open" and "Hawaii shooting" and "Liverpool vs Man United" and "Jennifer Aniston." The words "coronavirus" or "COVID-19" did not appear on the front page of the *New York Times*, which instead offered stories about an Angolan entrepreneur who'd built a shell empire, a story about the phenomenon of vanishing Native American women, and the President's impeachment trial. Very few people in the United States, it seemed, were talking about the virus. Nobody I knew had been. Neither had I. When I hadn't been designing assignments for my spring graduate course, or trying to write or read, or riding my bike, or planning my family's evening meals, I'd been talking to anybody who would listen about the lights that had been appearing after dark in the woods where my father lived, a stone's throw from our family cemetery, on a hundred acres of wilderness bordering national forest in the mountains of Western North Carolina. Nobody knew what to make of them.

One month before, on December 21, 2019—the longest night of the year—I was taking a post-sunset walk, following an asphalt trail that meandered through the nearby municipal golf course adjacent to my neighborhood, toward the top of a hill that happened to be the highest point in the town of Blacksburg, Virginia, a spot that allowed visitors to view, during the daylight hours, the icons of our little town: the football stadium, the turret of the colossal administration building, the coal plant, the futuristic-looking arts center, and distant mountain ridges. My wife and son also enjoyed this view, but I usually took these walks alone, to clear my head after a long day of teaching and reading and writing, or simply to get some fresh air. Hours earlier, I'd attended a Virginia Tech basketball game with my friend Robert and his thirteen-year-old son Felix, the latter of whom had floated an idea he'd heard a YouTuber endorse: that, as the Mayans had predicted, the universe had ended in 2012. We were now living in a simulation, which explained why everything these days seemed so messed up. Admittedly, this was an intriguing theory to consider as I walked through the longest night of the year, which so far happened to be moonless. A smattering of stars appeared in the sky, clotted here and there with tufts of cloud drifting low enough to reflect the pinkish lights of the town center and the Virginia Tech campus.

So . . . convincing, I thought to myself.

I meant "the reality of it all."

Like, what I was seeing.

It all seemed so *believable.*

As had become my habit on these random walks of mine, I decided to call my father. For the previous three months since my mother had died, he'd been living by himself on a remote piece of property in the mountains of southwestern North Carolina, in the big brick house that he and Mom had moved into when I was sixteen. I'd often imagined—though he'd claimed this was not the case—that he might be lonely.

"Hello?" he said.

"Hey," I said. "What am I interrupting?"

That was his line, the one he used whenever he called me.

"Well," he replied. "I've been meaning to tell you. Some weird stuff's been happening."

This wasn't news. Weird stuff had been happening for a while. The weirdest of all? My mother, at the improbably young age of seventy-three, had died. Even though I'd been there to help lower her coffin into the grave in our family cemetery—a clearing in the woods behind my parents' house on land that my grandparents had originally purchased nearly forty years before—I often caught myself wondering: *Where did she go?* Everyone who'd known her had come to accept, more or less, how she would die—she'd been diagnosed with dementia in her mid-60s, and then Alzheimer's, and then, finally, Parkinson's—but the fact of her disappearance seemed no less incomprehensible. You see, once upon a time, my mother had been a dynamo. She whipped up extravagant meals, canned vegetables, baked bread, tended to flowers, managed finances and my father's dental office, served as leader for the so-called "fruit program" that sold boxes of Florida citrus to local town folk in order to raise funds for our local church school, practiced the hymns she would play on the piano for church on Saturday morning, led religious educational classes for young children, corresponded with family members and distant friends, made trips to visit her parents and siblings in upstate South Carolina, refilled hummingbird feeders, read her Bible, drank cups of instant coffee, ate chocolate chip cookies, and laughed. Everyone in my family—on both sides—expected that she'd be the last to go: that, as they wilted into the fragilities of senescence, she would be taking care of *them*. A decade before, it would've been impossible for any of our family members to imagine that she'd slowly expire three months before her seventy-fourth birthday. Of course, years before that, she'd stopped becoming herself. We all missed the versions of my mother before she'd disappeared for good. Once she was gone, we simply missed the person she'd always been: daughter, friend, sister, wife, mother. As her eldest son, her disappearance imbued me with a new superpower: by imagining her standing in her kitchen, long before she could've had the wherewithal to imagine her future demise, I could make myself cry.

I was therefore at all times and anywhere thirty seconds away from tears.

For two nights, my father said, he'd looked out his bedroom window, down the grassy hill to the pond and to a nearby mountain ridge. There, in the woods, he'd observed a number of lights—in various places—flashing. A light would appear and disappear as quickly: bright, brief flashes. A few seconds later, others would appear somewhere else. According to my father, these lights never moved. That is, he had not been able to observe them *as* they moved. He'd only been able to perceive how they'd reappeared in different locations, giving the impression that there were either many lights or one single source that reignited after repositioning itself.

His first explanation? Coon hunters. Even so: he hadn't heard any dogs. And what was also strange? The flashes hadn't behaved like flashlights. Hadn't appeared as beams. Hadn't swung through the dark. They'd simply flashed very quickly on and off. Like mysterious signals. Or, and this seemed more likely, like the result of pranksters playing elaborate and unkind tricks. My father had considered driving his Highlander down the road to get closer. He'd imagined retracting his sunroof and firing a shotgun into the air. I didn't ask why, though I supposed he'd figured this might serve as a kind of warning. A shotgun, he'd assured me, fired skyward, wouldn't hurt anybody.

"I could be standing on the porch," he said, "and you could be down by the pond, and I could shoot at you with a shotgun, and nothing would happen."

"We should try it," I said.

"Maybe on one of my grandchildren first."

I laughed. "So, now what?"

He didn't know. He'd gotten to sleep the night before by convincing himself the lights had been the result of wind-jostled branches scraping against power lines and causing sparks, but the next morning, he'd thought *no* and disparaged this idea as "dumb." He'd walked to the place where, according to his estimation, the lights had appeared. There, he followed a trail winding to the ridgetop. He hadn't found anything, though he'd confirmed something he'd already known: the woods were too densely tangled to negotiate properly. In addition to trees, the forest housed too many vines and briars and rhododendrons for anyone to navigate at the speed the flashes would have required. He couldn't say what he'd seen. Even so, he'd convinced himself of one thing for sure: the lights were not human in origin.

"Maybe," I suggested, "it's Mom trying to get in touch with us."

Dad ignored me. He knew that I knew he didn't believe in ghosts. His religion wouldn't allow it. My father had no other choice, on the first day of winter, and the longest night of the year, but to keep watch and to wait.

I've always known that my father was famous in our town—and beyond—because he was a very good dentist, and also that he was not like any of the other dentists that I knew. And, as it turned out, I knew an absurd number of dentists. My grandfather—my mother's father—had been a dentist, and one of his sons had been a dentist. My mother's youngest sister had married a dentist. Two of my cousins became dentists; another of my cousins married one. And because my father had gone to dental school, many of his classmates, who remained some of his best friends, also worked as dentists, and their wives were often or had been, like my own mother before she'd had children, dental hygienists. And because the denomination to which the vast majority of our family members pledged allegiance—the Seventh-day Adventist church—had been shaped, at least in part, in opposition to mainstream society, and because its founders had seen fit to organize the construction of its own educational institutions, and had thereby manufactured its own idiosyncratic and insular culture and society, one that was interested in both spreading the gospel and maintaining the very good health of its members, as well as its fellow humans, many people who'd been raised in the church and had matriculated through its elementary, secondary, and advanced educational institutions became pastors or teachers or medical professionals. Of those medical professionals, a great many became physicians. A great many also became dentists.

Unlike other dentists I knew, my father did not drive expensive cars or play the stock market. He did not, despite the suggestions of health care management professionals, avoid making friends with his staff, but instead became a kind of father figure to the women—affectionately called "the girls" by both my parents—who worked for him: a confidant in whom they trusted for advice about boyfriends, ex-husbands, kids, and managing credit card debt. For years, he drove a beat-up Ford truck, the inside of which was littered with magazine inserts, dirt clods, packets of stale Trident sugar-free gum, mint-flavored dental floss, and cardboard boxes of rubber gloves. His shoes—and most of his clothes— he'd been cycling through for decades. Unlike other dentists, who packed as many patients into a day as possible, my father did not hurry. He had no quotas, and for many years avoided thinking about money to the extent that if a patient couldn't or simply refused to pay, he declined to track them down. He worked slowly. Patiently. Carefully. He tapped gently on gumlines to test whether Novocain had taken effect and, if necessary, repeated injections. Patients often exited his office with drooling mouths stuffed with bloody gauze, dazed by the fact that they hadn't felt a thing. I'd witnessed that kind of scene unfold a hundred times. As a kid, I'd spent entire days in that office, watching *I Dream of Jeannie* and *Bewitched* on a tiny television suspended from the bottom of a cupboard in the dental lab, where the girls stirred impression mixture in flexible green bowls or visited the fridge to pour shots of

Diet Pepsi into Dixie cups. Periodically, my father would call me to an examination room, saying, "I'd like you to meet my girlfriend," and there, beaming in the dental chair, would be a little old lady whose gnarled hands squeezed his.

My father was an indiscriminate flirt, and his patients—men, women, and children—all loved being at the center of his attention. They brought him sacks of tomatoes and okra and corn and potatoes. Jars of honey. Venison jerky. Hand-carved walking sticks. Quilts. Knives with pearlescent handles. Jellied rhubarb in jars with stickered lids that recorded the dates of the canning in scrawling cursive. Buckeyes, for good luck. He befriended bulldozer operators, postal clerks, high school teachers, retirees from Florida, ex-Olympians, ex-cons, masseuses, farmers, real estate agents, mechanics, prisoners in leg-irons, sheriffs, deputies, drug addicts, covert marijuana farmers, lawyers, carpenters, pharmacists, and conspiracy-theory-peddling militiamen. There was the bank teller who'd never been caught without makeup, not even when she mowed her lawn. The old nun who, at Christmastime, maintained a manger outside her apartment door with flashing lights and stuffed animals. The overalled millionaire who owned one of the planet's largest land-clearing companies. The ruddy, big-cheeked, pot-bellied man who rode a moped and claimed to be the first cousin of Xavier Roberts, inventor of the Cabbage Patch Kids doll. The one-eared man who kept a dried-up "bear pussy" in his billfold, which, according to my father, was "a wad of dried-up skin and hair." The jailer who relayed stories about the kinds of objects that female prisoners had stuffed up their respective buttholes: a carton of cigarettes, in one instance, an entire bedsheet, in another.

I'd always known that I'd never be as good a person as my father. I had also known, because I'd listened closely to the stories that my father had told, that he'd felt the same way about his father, and that his father had felt the same about his. By "good" I mean everything that the word could possibly connote: that I'd never learn how to properly match the depths of my father's selflessness; that I'd not be as patient or skilled, and therefore not as successful at whatever job I ended up doing; that I'd never be able to mimic his quick and improvisational wit, would never learn how to affectionately antagonize with jokey insults the kind of men he met at the barber shop or the hardware store; that I'd never have the balls to ride a motorcycle with reckless precision or pick up an opossum by its tail; that I'd never perfect, as he somehow had, despite how dorky he looked employing it, his fabled "skyhook" basketball shot; that I'd never learn how to catch rainbow trout with my bare hands. Had I ever asked my father to produce a list of things his own father had done better or more competently, I have no doubt he would've cobbled together a just-as-long list, because if the sons in my father's side of the family had one thing in common, if we could be said to lay claim to a single tradition, it was that we all felt completely overshadowed by the legacies of our fathers—and whether we acknowledged it or not, this fact became part of the reason why the idea of a "heavenly Father" had come so naturally to us: our fathers, as forces of strength and understanding and beneficence, were the first deities we'd ever known. Of course, we wouldn't have said that our fathers were our "first gods," wouldn't have even allowed ourselves to think in such blasphemous terms, but whether we acknowledged it or not, it was true: in the mythologies produced by members of our family, our fathers were our Lords. Unlike the fabled Old Testament Lord, however, they had not asked to be worshipped, nor set the terms of how and when they were to be adored. We worshipped them anyway. These fathers were not only nicer and kinder and more generous than most people we knew, but they also represented the best possible versions of the word "father" or even "person" we could imagine. Whatever defects they might have been said to possess had been secreted away or, more likely, never existed in the first place. Had I been pressed to admit it, I would've been forced to confess that the only "faults" I could find in my own father were superficial, and the fact that I categorized "physical diminishments" as "faults"—my father had a receding hairline and wore bifocals—was evidence of my own inherent unkindness, and therefore, my own inferiority.

As my wife Kelly sometimes says to me, in reference to my own less-than-acceptable behavior, "Jim Vollmer would never act that way."

Not that I'm a particularly bad father. I'd drawn *Ren and Stimpy* cartoons on notes in Elijah's lunchbox, taken him to the movies, driven him all over southwestern Virginia for soccer games, showered him with gifts and toys I'd spent hours researching online, and shot baskets with him in the driveway. But I would never—as my father had once done—drive five hours to a college apartment in Chapel Hill and then five hours back to retrieve a laptop my child had forgotten when returning home for spring break. I could never have claimed, as my father could've, to rarely if ever have raised my voice at my child. And who knows what kind of damage I'd inflicted by treating my one-and-only like a little brother: never let him beat me in backyard soccer games, cursed when he scored more goals in FIFA on the PlayStation. As a toddler in his crib, I'd once tried to convince him that he should stop crying, because the monsters in the attic—the door to which was only feet from his bed—could smell his tears. The point is: I haven't always put my family's needs before my own. I can be selfish and sulky. Antagonistic and rude.

In a snapshot from the early '70s, my father wears a round helmet glowing with a corona of reflected sunlight, and straddles a motorcycle as it flies over a sand dune. He's always been a showoff. A daredevil. He crashed at least a dozen cars before he turned twenty. Taught himself to barefoot ski, pop wheelies in wheelchairs, grab venomous snakes by the tails. But his favorite trick—and the one that both disturbed and pleased a crowd—involved balancing a baby at the end of his outstretched hand. The stunt required one infant, preferably between three and six months: one who'd yet to learn how to stand up on her own. Gripping the baby's tiny socked feet, my father would balance her in an outstretched arm. A broom steadied stick-end on the tip of a finger could achieve a similar effect but would've been far less dramatic, especially when, once my father had exhausted either his own strength or the tolerance of the baby's parents for this particular stunt, he allowed the child to fall from her place on his palm into his other arm. The babies loved it! They'd beam and coo, as if proud to have enjoyed the sensation of standing.

As if they had known that my father had helped them do something amazing.

My father also helped my mother execute something amazing: he helped her die with dignity. It was no easy feat, even if you were the World's Most Patient Man. Because here's the thing: if and when you lose your mind, the whole world slowly goes dark. At night, windows become opaque and reflect twisted apparitions. You can't say what you want because as soon as you start your sentence, you've forgotten what you wanted to say; the words vanish in your mind and your mouth downshifts to mumble. Forget writing, you can't figure out how to use a pen. Nobody knows what's going through your mind, but the consensus seems to lie somewhere between "not much" and "probably more than we can imagine." In the end, you can't walk without help. Other things you can't do by yourself: use the bathroom, shower, or eat. If you're lucky, though, you have a life partner. A husband. A lover. A person who talks to you in the same bemused and adoring ways that he always has. Who makes fun of you because he knows you always enjoyed being teased. Because you've always liked to laugh, especially at yourself. "I just cain't he'p it," you used to say, before you needed a napkin around your neck when you ate. Back when you'd dance poorly but with vigor: biting your lip and flapping your arms like chicken wings, laughing because this made your husband turn his face away and cover his eyes with his hands. It was ridiculous. You knew it was. That's why you did it. You were bringing joy into the world. And filling every room you entered with laughter. And love. And light.

No one on earth could've taken better care of my mother than my father. As the recognizable parts of her began to disappear, my father, in an attempt to preserve, as far as was possible, the particulars of the life with which he had grown accustomed, had taught himself, among other things, to cook and bake the things that Mom had cooked and baked, and therefore became quite adept in the running of their household. He taught himself how to make her homemade bread. Her soups: vegetable, tomato cabbage, potato. Her vegetarian meatloaf casserole. He canned applesauce. Sent me messages on Facebook, through the account that belonged to my mother. Whenever I received a message from "Sandra Gilbert Vollmer," I knew it'd been my father who'd sent it. He lacked the power to change the name on the account. That password disappeared the day my mother forgot it.

It's impossible to say how my mother experienced her demise. In her heyday, she was so effortlessly and vivaciously herself. And stunningly beautiful. Imagine Uma Thurman with smaller eyes and softer features. Furiously industrious, my mother baked and cooked and canned and gardened and swept and scrubbed and laundered and sewed and painted. Her pantry, fridge, and freezers were always stocked: jars of applesauce and strawberry jam, sliced and frozen loaves of homemade bread, sacks of semi-sweet morsels, cans of Campbell's alphabet soup, tubs of vanilla ice cream, cases of A&W root beer for Saturday night floats.

For the majority of four very formative years of my life—ages 14 to 18, when I was attending Georgia-Cumberland

Academy, a Seventh-day Adventist boarding school in the heart of north Georgia—I lived without my parents. I spent summers at home, and during the school year visited them periodically (once a month, usually), and I spoke with them often enough on the pay phones in my dormitory's lobby, but they didn't often make appearances in my daily existence. The academy I attended wasn't the kind, I don't imagine, that the phrase "boarding school" might suggest to most people. There weren't brick walls or ivy or uniforms or rich people's kids. Tuition wasn't cheap, but if you couldn't afford it and counted yourself a member of our denomination, you could go; the Worthy Student fund at your local church would pitch in. Plus, everyone who attended school there— no matter what their financial situation—had a job. We'd been told that one couldn't put a price on a Christian education, but somebody had to pay the bills, and—even if our parents had money enough to pay our tuition, which wasn't cheap—we had to help. We inserted time cards into time clocks. We prepared vats of pudding and spaghetti sauce. We sprayed hot water at trays students shoved through the dishwasher's window, used our gloved fingers to dig out the lentil loaf and green beans and mashed potatoes some a-hole had stuffed into a plastic tumbler. We squeegeed oily flesh smears from windows, answered phones, scribbled messages we'd never deliver. We skimmed algae from the sewage pond. We hosed down buses. We mowed. We soldered stained glass at a warehouse beside the duck pond, sewed cushions for lawn chairs at the factory at the edge of the campus. Work would teach us dignity, humility, and the value of a dollar: We kept a small portion, to buy candy and caffeine-free soda at the dorm store or Taco Bell during weekly town trips, but most of what we earned went to our bills. The rest was tithe and, because we feared what'd happen if we took what was rightfully God's, we'd checked the box during registration that said, "Yes, I want to return ten percent."

But what we didn't have? Parents. Parents were so absent from daily life at Georgia-Cumberland Academy that I often found myself wondering if my classmates even had them. I knew it wasn't possible but for some kids it was simply beyond my imaginative capabilities to dream them up. Much easier to imagine they had hatched from eggs or been dropped by storks into the world. Maybe it was because we lacked the requisite information. Most kids didn't talk about their parents. Didn't hang photos of them on their walls. But it wasn't just parents who were absent. The world outside our school might not have existed at all. It certainly had no bearing on our day-to-day activities which were: breakfast, chapel, classes, work, rec period, chapel, study hall, and bed.

I had always known, from the time that I could conceive of and imagine such a thing as "secondary education," that I would, at age 14, pack up my belongings and go away to boarding school, where I would live not with my family but a group of boys and girls who had been raised more or less like I had. Nearly everyone in my family had gone—for at least some length of time—to boarding school, as nearly every good Adventist child does. My grandfather on my mother's side—who, it was often cited, had left home with all of his earthly possessions inside a single shoebox—had met my grandmother at a boarding school in Fletcher, North Carolina; my own parents had begun their courtship at a boarding school just outside of Asheville. In many ways, I had been fated, before I'd been born, to attend some kind of Seventh-day Adventist boarding school, and by going—or so I often imagined, once I got old enough to speculate about the particulars—I would fulfill my destiny.

It turned out—and hey, fun fact—it didn't matter if you surrendered your Walkman and/or all your cassettes, or your television, or your knives and firecrackers, or your D&D, or your porn, or your GameBoy, or your fantasy novels, and it didn't matter if you sang "As the deer panteth for the water, so my soul longeth for thee" first thing in the morning and then studied "The Story of Redemption" in Bible class later on, and then gathered with every boy in the dorm chapel again after rec period and then attended vespers on Friday night and church on Saturday, and assembled around the flagpole at campus center for "eventide" on Saturday night— if you lived in a dorm with ninety other teenage boys, your environment was guaranteed to be less than wholesome, and it would often reek of rotten sweat socks, burrito farts, and Drakkar Noir. It was true that certain of my fellow hallmates held impromptu Bible studies in the dorm lobby, while others kept their rooms meticulously clean, or happily spent evenings ironing shirts or dutifully folding laundry, but for the most part, the boys living with me in my dorm went wild every chance we got. We fired squirt bottles of bleach at each other, popped our best friends in their sacks when they least expected it. We put each other in headlocks and leglocks. We threw punches. To a select few, we revealed our stashes of forbidden goods we'd smuggled in and kept hidden, in secret locations in our rooms we often admired as ingenious:

a case of Coca-Cola, a single smoke bomb, a *Master of Puppets* cassette whose lettering had been scraped off (thus preventing it from being identified as contraband), a set of homemade nunchucks fashioned out of sawed-off pieces of broomstick, a couple ripped-out pages from the November 1988 issue of *Penthouse* (stowed inside a *TIME* magazine bearing the bust of Mikhail Gorbachev). We locked ourselves in bathroom stalls and wept; we stayed on our side of the room and refused to speak unless spoken to. The loneliest of us emitted only the softest and shortest of sounds, saving our voices for calls home on the pay phones—fifteen-minute slots we had to sign up for, during which we'd suppress the urge to beg our parents to retrieve us, because, more than anything, we wanted to go home.

What I also wanted to be more than anything? To be a boy with a girlfriend. I knew that my parents had boyfriends and girlfriends at their boarding school, Mount Pisgah Academy, and that my father had gotten in trouble for sneaking into a girl's dorm room to make out with her and that my mother had gotten in trouble for smooching with a guy named Ronnie in a piano practice room, but I also knew that Mom and Dad had begun dating each other at their boarding school. As had my mother's parents. My grandfather liked to tell the story about seeing my grandmother, as a new student, walk into the chapel while the school was hosting a President's Day program and noting her new gloves and blue sweater, thought to himself: that's the one. I'd spent my elementary school years in a two-room school of thirty kids in grades one through eight.

One thing for sure: the students at Georgia-Cumberland Academy had no clue what was going on in the world beyond. We had been deprived of so many things—cassette players, rock and roll, video games, *Dungeons & Dragons*, caffeinated drinks, meat, radios, jewelry, and TV, which meant that, for the most part, we had little way of knowing what was happening outside our campus borders, which, under no conditions, were we to wander beyond, at least not without permission and a faculty sponsor. We'd heard that the Berlin Wall had come down, but we only had the vaguest ideas of what that could mean. We knew when the Gulf War started because the boys' Dean rolled the TV into the TV room, and we watched CNN's coverage of the bombing of Baghdad, and felt maybe a twinge of national pride due to the expressed might of our superior military. As a rule, however, we did not watch TV. Though newspapers were available, hanging from wooden sticks in the library, we rarely read them. We didn't subscribe to *TIME* or *People* or *Sports Illustrated*. We'd lost track of prime-time TV shows, couldn't tell you what was new or what the #1 song on Top Forty was—and yet, we didn't feel as if we were being deprived. We were, more often than not, happy not to know. We had no problem existing outside of time.

Three months before I talked to my father about the blinking lights in his woods, I'd been riding my bike along the bottom of a valley below the plateau where I lived, in Blacksburg, Virginia. It was nearly 9 a.m. on September 11, 2019. I was seven miles from home, a ride that would necessitate a thousand-foot climb. My phone vibrated in the side pocket of my cycling jersey. I pulled onto the shoulder. The screen said *Dad*. I swiped to answer. A woman's voice greeted me.

"Matthew?"

"Yes."

"Hi. This is Tina. Your dad wanted me to call you to let you know that your mother has just passed."

This wasn't a surprise. I'd known this was coming. But I couldn't tell how, in that moment, I felt.

Tina, a petite, long-haired woman who wore ankle-length skirts and whose previous job had something to do with a self-sufficient boarding school, had served as my mother's primary caretaker for the last couple of months: moving mom from her bed to the wheelchair, from the wheelchair to toilet, toilet to wheelchair, wheelchair to a remote-controlled recliner in the front room (where a television played reruns of *The Andy Griffith Show* or *Perry Mason*), tying a napkin around her neck and feeding her what little she'd eat, talking to her, brushing her hair, and taking her out to the porch so she could feel the sun on her face.

"Your dad's pretty emotional," she said. "He'd like you and your sister to come as soon as you can."

I thanked Tina and hung up. I called my wife to tell her the news and ask her to drive from Blacksburg to the Deli Mart at the corner of Luster's Gate and Den Hill Road. Otherwise, it would have taken me thirty minutes to climb to the top of the mountain, and I didn't want to lose that much time.

Even though I kept hearing Tina's voice in my head—*your mother has passed*—I didn't know what to think or how to feel. I wondered how long it took for a body to decompose and realized I had no idea. It'd been ridiculously hot for September. And dry. Other than a stray thunderstorm, the southeastern United States hadn't received sustained rain for weeks. I knew my mother would not be embalmed before she was buried and I worried—and I realize now that this was kind of ridiculous—that her body might somehow deteriorate before I reached her.

Your mother has passed. I tried to remember the line from *The Stranger* by Albert Camus. But I couldn't. As simple as the sentence was—"Maman died today"—I was unable to retrieve it. *Come as soon as you can.*

All I knew was that, for the first time in my life, I was alive in the world without my mother. The disease had won. The kindest, most unselfish, sweetest, most loving person I had ever met had finally been erased from the world.

A month later, my father texted to say that he'd spent an hour and a half on the phone with "the Social Security people." Apparently, there had been a mix up: the government thought my father—not my mother—was the one who had died. The actual sentence my father had typed was, *They made a mistake and I'm dead instead of your mom.* He followed this news with a yellow emoji with a rectangle of gritted teeth, a graph-like mouth indicative of a grimace.

Still not straightened out, he added.

This is what you get for taking over Mom's Facebook account, I said.

No response.

Also, I texted. *That's insane.*

Nothing.

I tried another approach: *So, what are you gonna do to prove Mom's dead and you're not?*

A speech bubble appeared. Three appearing and disappearing dots began cycling.

Show up at their office with a death certificate for Sandra and a photo ID for me. And a stethoscope.

I told him that he should wear zombie makeup and limp to the front desk murmuring, "Me still alive. For most part." I've been telling patients, he replied, that I hope they don't mind being worked on by a dead man.

Two years before, my father had texted me a picture of an unvarnished wooden coffin, classically heptagonal in shape, accompanied by a message that said: *My casket's almost finished.* I zoomed in. I frowned. It seemed wrong for my father to have used the word "casket" to describe what was clearly a "coffin." To make sure, I typed "difference between casket and coffin" into a search engine. I learned that "coffins are tapered at the head and foot and are wide at the shoulders" and that "caskets are rectangular in shape and are usually constructed of better-quality timbers and feature higher standards of workmanship."

So "coffin" it was.

My father's coffin was pale and smoothly sanded. In the photo, it sat upon a concrete floor. In the background, a garage door of ribbed metal suggested that the coffin was living, for now, in someone's workshop. My father had simultaneously texted this same image and message to my sister, Carrie, who'd replied only with the word, "Umm," signaling—or so I presumed—a hesitancy to consider such an object with the same nonchalance with which my father announced its existence, since looking at his casket—or coffin—would inevitably summon the image of him lying dead inside it, awaiting burial in our family plot.

My father was not sick, or feeble, or impaired. He certainly didn't look seventy years old; he possessed the kind of youthful exuberance that inspired him to carry ten grocery bags at once, or backflip into the freshwater trout pond in front of his house after an afternoon of grass mowing. Though he no longer occupied the so-called "prime" of his life, and though he had a heart condition that required the taking of a daily medication, and a liver disease that necessitated he drink vast quantities of water, he was in good health, exercising moderately, and subsisting on a mostly vegetarian, legume-heavy diet. If one of his patients asked him when he was going to retire, he'd likely evade the question by saying that he'd been enjoying his work as a dentist now more than ever. After all, he'd been taking fewer patients and working fewer hours, giving himself more time to work on extractions and fillings, and to socialize with the amusingly idiosyncratic parade of characters that showed up in the theaters of his examination rooms. More significantly, I supposed that going to work, for my father, had been a way of exiting, if only momentarily, the reality of his home life, which, thanks to the slow and steady deletion of my mother's capabilities, had been utterly transformed.

Although it had been alarming to see a photo of my father's nearly finished coffin, it had not been surprising. My father's mother had also requested that a friend of the family build her a coffin, and once he'd finished, she paid it a visit. There, in our friend's garage, the lid was removed, and my grandmother climbed aboard, and lay down inside, cooing delightedly. She loved it. She suspected she would be very comfortable there, even though she'd believed all her life that death was nothing but a dreamless sleep, and without question could've quoted from memory what the writer of Ecclesiastes had said about dying, that "the living know that they shall die, but the dead know not anything." Eventually, my grandmother would expire after succumbing to a long and relentless illness, the same one that my mother would battle, and that might one day afflict me, assuming that the medical world would have failed to discover a cure. And when my grandmother finally did end up dying, at her home, the men of the family gathered at her bedside and wrapped her body in a quilt, and placed her in the selfsame coffin she'd commissioned, and hauled her through a spring blizzard to the family plot, lowering her into the freshly dug grave, opened that morning in the clearing behind my parents' house, next to my grandfather, and three dogs: a place where, I knew, as a kid, that the members of my father's side of the family would be buried, and where, on Resurrection Day, we would spring from our graves, which, after all, were merely temporary beds for our sleeping souls to rest.

My family spent many a Saturday afternoon on the property where our cemetery is located. My grandparents bought the land in 1982, following my grandfather's retirement from medicine, and that's what we called it back then: "the Land."

I'm going up to the Land, my father would say. *Anybody wanna visit the Land?*

The answer, for me, was usually: yes and no. The Land was cool and all but it was incredibly remote: a teeming jungle of spiderwebbed thickets, massive overhanging slabs of lime-stone, solemn stands of hemlock, and rushing streams with waterfalls and natural rock slides and deep, spectral pools. The Land was beautiful, private, and—because of the thick foliage—dark. Peering into those woods always gave me a lonely feeling, and it was easy to imagine that peril would befall me should I venture too far inside.

To reach the Land, we followed the old two-lane that bisected the valley where our town had been built and traveled a few miles west until we reached the local airport, surrounded by corn fields whose tilled earth yielded ancient pottery and chunks of arrowheads left by the Cherokee three hundred years before. At the airport, we turned right onto another two-lane road, wound alongside a roaring creek, and forked right onto a gravel drive until it turned to nothing more than a rotten gash in jungle-thick woods. In these woods, there were bears and wild hogs and snakes, the latter with which I had firsthand experience: once, while hiking with my parents and sister, I had stepped on a copperhead that my father subsequently beat to death with his walking stick, marveling afterwards that it hadn't bitten me. Surely, he'd said, my guardian angel had shut the mouth of that serpent. I remembered how Daniel's angels had closed the mouths of the lions in that famous den of yore, and imagined mine grabbing the fat head of the viper and squeezing the bejeezus out of it.

Eventually, my grandparents cleared a plot on the Land and built a house next to a creek where, if you looked hard and long enough, you might spot a rainbow trout, and where, if you were me, carrying a Mason jar of fish food, you'd slip and break the jar and end up with a shard piercing your arm: a little mouth of blood and fat your father would sew up in the lab of his dental office. Years later, my parents took the road to my grandparents' house a little farther and built a house of their own, a massive rectangle of brick and stone. And a short walk beyond their backyard: a clearing in the woods where our family would begin to bury its dead.

The vast majority of people who I've told about the blinking lights in the woods surrounding my father's house have had the same response.

"It's obvious," they've said. "Those lights? That's your mom."

It was a nice thing to imagine: my beloved mother sending beneficent signals—like a ghostly Morse code—from another dimension. Such a story might've comforted the members of my family, supposing they could've brought themselves to believe such a thing. But they couldn't. It would've been a different story if everybody in my family—aside from two uncles and a handful of cousins—hadn't belonged to the same denomination: the Seventh-day Adventist church. You see, members of this church were not under any circumstances allowed to believe in ghosts. If you told an Adventist that you'd been visited by a long-lost loved one—or claimed to have witnessed a supernatural phenomenon of any kind—you were likely to receive one of two responses: either your mind was playing tricks on you, or you were being targeted by demonic forces. Either way, there was only one prescription for someone who'd been visited by a phantom. Get down on your knees, and start praying. Until you could decide whether you were crazy or Satan-adjacent.

I also did not, as a former Adventist, believe in ghosts. Or, more accurately: I didn't think I did. Honestly, I had no idea. I liked to quote the first few lines of the *Dhammapada*, a collection of sayings attributed to the Buddha:

"We are what we think. / All that we are arises with our thoughts. / With our thoughts we make the world."

In other words, whatever human beings might be said to believe was the product of the stories they told and the stories they believed. This wasn't a secret. Fake news, deep fakes, AI-generated internet ads, social media "bubbles," and all manner of conspiracy theories had contributed to an environment in which nearly any belief could be validated or denied. The longer I lived, the less certain I felt about any so-called "beliefs" I might ever lay claim to. That said, I often thought that one of the best decisions I'd ever made, during my freshman year of college, when I was eighteen years old and living in a tiny apartment in central Massachusetts with a friend from high school and found myself facing, for the first time in my life, the decision to go to church on a Saturday morning or not and, maybe because I knew no authority figure would be standing in the back with a clipboard placing checkmarks beside names, as they had been for the last four years at the Seventh-day Adventist boarding school I'd attended, I'd simply chosen not to go. And even though I felt like I might be doing something wrong, I also felt a sense of liberation. And so, the next week I made the same decision. And the next. And the next. Until I reached a point of no return.

And I simply never went back.

"I just stopped going": this is what I often tell people if they ask me how I "got out of" or "left" the Seventh-day Adventist church. Although I like the simplicity of this answer, it's actually a lot more complicated than that. At some point, I know, I reached a saturation point. I'd gotten tired. Tired of the patriarchal hierarchy, which disallowed women from serving as ordained ministers and church leaders, and which even my father, who had nothing against women serving as dentists or physicians or leadership positions in other non-church organizations, supported. Tired of people insisting that the language of scripture should always be read literally—and linearly. Tired of smug, overconfident pastors, who might have remembered more Bible verses than I had—but not alternate ways of reading them. And more than maybe anything, tired of hearing about "the End." How many church members before me had spent the majority of their lives looking toward a future event that they believed themselves to be on the verge of experiencing—but never actually had? How much time and energy had been spent by evangelists and pastors decoding present day events using the lenses of apocalyptic literature written in the first century? The promises of Adventist "Revelation Seminars"—*Reveal hidden Bible truths! Unlock biblical truths! Time is running out for planet Earth! Startling Prophecies for America! Revelation's Ancient Discoveries Reveal the Future! Finally, the Truth about the Origins of the Universe! Lies Exposed! Mysteries Solved! Answers found!* —rang hollow to my ears; the sensational headlines sounded to me like scare tactics, superficially transparent strategies used by advertisers desperate to sell their products: in this case, the answer key to a book that had been dictated to ancient prophets by God himself. According to Adventism, life was a test, and if you took the final exam without having studied, it could be the difference between eternal life and eternal death.

Simply put, I couldn't help but imagine existence was bigger—and more mysterious—than what I'd been taught to believe.

Eventually, my father, while observing the lights, took a video with his phone.

"You need to watch it in a dark room," he said. "Look to the right of the middle of the screen. The first couple are bright. The rest are faint."

Finally, I thought. *Evidence.*

I entered a closet, shut the door, and tapped the red triangle. The screen was black. I could faintly—but only just barely—observe the jagged outline of trees along a distant ridgeline. About ten seconds in, the first light appeared: an unmistakable LED-bright flash, the quickest pin prick of light, like a firefly in fast-forward. A few others followed: nearly imperceptible, millisecond-long bursts of light. And then the video went dark.

Nobody in my family had ever given me the impression that death was something to fear. In Adventist theology, people didn't go to heaven when they died. They didn't go to hell. They didn't get reincarnated or wander the earth as ghosts. They simply stopped being conscious. Or, to put it another, tautological way: when people died, they *died*. This was, I knew, a belief unique to our denomination, and was part of many others—including our belief that Saturday was the true day of Christian worship, a conviction that dictated we observe the Jewish Sabbath, from the hours of sundown Friday to sundown Saturday—that made our church "peculiar." Adventists didn't fear eternal hellfire because they knew that those infernal caverns and horned creatures wielding pitchforks, as so often depicted in popular culture, were nothing but deceptions, cooked up by Satan himself to instill fear and doubt in the minds of humans, and to besmirch the

character of the Almighty, who, if he could be said to maintain the upkeep of an eternal hellfire, would have to perform
an ongoing miracle to continue to keep humans, who, after
all, were quite flammable, burning forever. And what kind
of God would that be? Certainly not a kind or loving one.

As a child, I found this belief—that once a person died,
they were, in fact, dead—quite comforting. I remember taking
a smug pleasure in denigrating the portrayals I encountered
in cartoons or funny pages of supposedly dead people, who
were frequently drawn as transparent angels playing harps
or standing, in their robes and halos, atop fluffy clouds.
Such depictions I recognized as fictional. Despite what many
gospel songs might have insisted, God did not call people
home to heaven because he needed additional voices for His
choir. Nor was anyone no matter how despicably they'd led
their lives—crying out for mercy in fiery caverns while horned
demons jabbed the arrow-tipped prongs into their buttocks.
Nor were the righteous dead looking down upon us from
paradise; keeping watch over the rest of living humanity
would mean that the dead could be said to know *something*,
and we Adventists knew, thanks to Ecclesiastes 9:5, that
what they actually knew was *nothing*. Therefore, the idea that
a dead loved one had taken up residence in heaven was not
only "not true," it was "unbiblical." Adventist pastors often
went so far as to point out during sermons that the notion
of a dead person passing from this world directly into heaven
bore at least some relation to the first lie ever told, way back
in the Garden of Eden, when the serpent promised Eve
that, should she to eat of the forbidden fruit, she would *not
surely die*. Furthermore, these same pastors often reminded
us, wasn't heaven supposed to be without tears and sorrow?
How could my grandfather, for instance, the beloved family

31

physician, look upon this sorry old world and do anything but shed tears? No way. Pa-paw was, like the rest of the dead, *dead*. Or, more specifically, *asleep*. And those sleeping in the loving mercy of the Lord Jesus' forgiveness would be awoken on the glorious day of his return.

So, my family? We weren't scared of death. And we weren't afraid to die.

But the process of dying? The whole suffering in agony part? That was something we would learn, over time, to fear.

"You'd do that for me wouldn't you? You'd put a pillow over my head, wouldn't you? For the old lady?"

This was something my paternal grandmother—the one who had moved to the Land and lived there, in the beginning, with my grandfather, and then alone, for over two decades after he died from complications following a stroke—used to say. It was a deal she'd made with me: if she ever lost her mind, she wanted me to put a pillow over her head until she suffocated, thus sparing her whatever indignities she supposed people who lost their minds had no choice but to endure.

Whether she ever thought about the psychological effects a grandson would suffer by having smothered his grandmother to death, I'll never know. She was too busy worrying about losing her mind. She'd witnessed her sister—a beloved music teacher and diabetic who always fed us Sugar Smacks and mint chocolate chip ice cream bars when we visited—transform from a hilarious, overweight, lovable loudmouth to a pale, shriveled, vacant-eyed shadow person. Furthermore, she was well-versed in performing the part of "pitiful old lady." My grandmother—we called her Honey because when her first grandbaby had been born, she was just vain enough to refuse to be called "grandma"—would often do this thing where she'd make her lower lip quiver, but because she wasn't, despite her resemblance to Lucille Ball, an actress, and because she hadn't fooled anybody in years, at least not since the 1950s when she'd killed my father's pet mice by secretly feeding them d-CON, claiming afterwards that they'd died of natural causes, I'd respond, as I usually did, to this request to smother her, as I usually did, with a deadpan, "Sure." Satisfied by this answer, she'd return to whatever she'd previously been doing, like watching *Oprah* at an ear-splitting volume or balancing her checkbook or frying something she liked to call a "savory egg sandwich." And then later, when she couldn't find her keys or her purse or the pen she'd been holding just moments before, I'd say, "Hup, looks like it's time for the pillow," or "Watch out, it's pillow time," and she'd drop her jaw as if horrified, and then she'd unleash this wild, high-pitched laugh.

It wasn't that Honey preferred to die by suffocation, but the idea of someone smashing a fat, feather-stuffed pillow over her face and holding it there until she stopped breathing and thrashing seemed like a far more reasonable way to go compared to the prospect of slowly becoming a stranger to herself, a fate she couldn't avoid by simply maintaining her health, which she'd most certainly done by exercising regularly and subsisting her entire life upon a vegetarian diet and laughing loudly and often. As long as I'd known her, people had complimented her appearance, insisting that she didn't look her age, and as far as I could tell, they'd been right. Blessed, for the most part, with a blithe spirit, she was a woman with a good figure and a pretty face and big round cheeks who sometimes ate candy and ice cream for dinner and who laughed, despite herself, at off-color jokes about flatulence or fat people or even the physically handicapped. She'd shout the name of the person who'd told the mean or dirty joke and say, "That's awful!" slap her knee, and laugh hysterically.

In the end, after all this talk about having someone—namely me—place a pillow over her head, and after all the jokes I'd made about it being time to "get the pillow," my grandmother *did* actually lose her mind, or at least enough of it so that she could no longer drive or cook or live by herself. It'd occurred to me that perhaps I should do what she'd asked me to so many times before, to put this dear old woman I loved out of her misery. And though I know it turned out sweetly in the end—she'd been moved out of *the* home and into *her* home to die, and after she drew her last breath, the men of the family placed her in the coffin she'd loved and carried it through a spring snow to the family cemetery, where it was lowered into a grave beside her husband's—I couldn't entirely let myself off the hook, and though I know she would've forgiven me for not having ever put a pillow over her head, she also might've understood if for her own benefit, for her own peace of mind, announced that it was time for the pillow and meant it, I had held it down until the storm of her resistance had expired, and everything had become like she'd always imagined, absolutely still.

II. A PECULIAR PEOPLE

Night after night, at the beginning of 2020, my father—sleeping in the same bed where my mother had died—woke up to use the bathroom: to be specific, he took a Mason jar from the side of the bed and peed into it. Why not? He now lived alone, and it was a lot easier than stumbling through the dark to reach the bathroom. Afterwards, he'd peer out his window. Sometimes he'd see something flash. Sometimes he wouldn't. But most nights? The lights were there. Blinking intermittently. Announcing their presence. Causing my dad's brow to furrow. And, because I wanted to see them myself, I made the five-hour trip from Virginia to North Carolina, to the cove deep in the mountains where he lived.

As a child, I knew that my church was made up of what my fellow congregants often referred to as "a peculiar people"—a group of believers that the world didn't seem to know much about. Seventh-day Adventists were rarely named or alluded to in media or popular culture. Adventist characters didn't make appearances on *Gilligan's Island* or *Good Times* or *The Cosby Show* or *Family Ties* or *A Different World* or *The Andy Griffith Show* or *The Walton's* or *Happy Days*. No athlete I followed counted himself as a member of the denomination. No famous singer sang about us. No comedian poked fun at our idiosyncrasies. No famous author listed our denomination in the bio on the back of his or her book. Aside from the 1984 story about Baby Fae—the infant into which Dr. Leonard Bailey, an Adventist doctor, had transplanted a baboon heart—we didn't show up in the news. I'd never watched a single movie that made so much as a fleeting reference to Seventh-day Adventists. (Though Adventists in theory welcome any-and-everyone in the world to join the church, the kind of person who ends up converting is much more particular; for instance, according to Bull and Lockhart's theory of the "revolving door," articulated in their sociological study of the Seventh-day Adventist church in their book *Seeking a Sanctuary*, the majority of converts to Adventism worldwide exist on a lower socioeconomic scale, while those who leave tend to inhabit a higher one.) I'd heard rumors that certain celebrities—namely Prince and Little Richard and Magic Johnson and Clifton Davis, the latter of whom played the pastor on the role of the TV show *Amen*, which also featured Sherman Helmsley from *The Jeffersons*—had been raised in the church, but I'd never been able to prove whether those rumors were true, and even if they had been, it wouldn't have mattered, because nobody—except gossipy SDA kids like me—gave a hoot. I knew that many of the cereals I enjoyed bore John Harvey Kellogg's surname, and that before he'd been "disfellowshipped" for espousing so-called "pantheistic" views, he'd been a member of the Adventist church; my great-grandfather's medical diploma from a school in Battle Creek, Michigan bore Kellogg's signature. I knew that Little Debbie snack cakes, of which I'd consumed an astounding number during my childhood, were made by the McKee family, and that the McKees were Adventists, and that, years ago, Mr. McKee had proposed to my grandmother, who—thankfully for all of us who wouldn't have existed had she said yes—turned him down. But that was it. It wasn't just that very few people knew much about Seventh-day Adventists. It was that nobody seemed to care. We weren't a mystery to be solved. We were a little strange, maybe, but not that strange. We didn't have giant polygamous families or wear magical underwear or refuse to celebrate birthdays. We didn't go out of our way to knock on people's doors. We didn't avoid doctors or medicine or blood transfusions. In fact, if you met one of us, it may very well have been at a hospital or physician's office. We may have taken a moment to pray with you. We may have given you a strange little book you never read because you found the diction archaic or the narrative kind of boring. You wouldn't have said we were pushy, though. You probably would've thought we were nice and described us as friendly. But you probably wouldn't have seen us again. And thus, we would've been almost immediately forgotten.

On only one occasion in over two decades of teaching at non-Adventist universities has a student ever admitted to having been raised in the church, and only one time out of twenty will a student have known someone who'd claimed to have been a Seventh-day Adventist, that person inevitably and tentatively raising his or her hand, while delivering an uncertain wince, saying something like "the name sounds familiar," and so then I explain, in as factual and as brief a way as possible, that the Seventh-day Adventist church was a denomination that emerged in the nineteenth century, during the Second Great Awakening, from what has been known as the Millerite Movement, when a preacher named William Miller, reading closely the books of Daniel and Revelation, and applying a sort of prophetic arithmetic to the numbers within these books, arrived at a conclusion: Jesus Christ would return to earth on October 22, 1844, a day that, for true believers, would afterwards be known as the Great Disappointment. It is here that my students—not all but definitely more than a few—often laugh.

At this point, I might admit that, from the perspective of a twenty-first century citizen looking back upon the expectations of delusional, heaven-sick folk living in the nineteenth century, that it might seem humorous at first, though I'd never thought it was that funny. Imagine, for instance, that you'd given away all your possessions, slaughtered your livestock and distributed the meat to the poor, all with the belief that you would be leaving this earth forever, to live in a paradise characterized by its lack of pain and suffering, and where you would spend eternity with God, solving all the mysteries of human existence. And then imagine that the day passes, and that the Son of God does not appear in the heavens. And that you have to go back to your regular life, the material wealth and comforts of which you had, for all practical purposes, completely abandoned.

Whatever I say about Adventism on these occasions, I do my best to provide a basic, bare-bones description: the Seventh-day Adventist church believes that Christians ought to be honoring the Jewish Sabbath, as outlined in Exodus 20:11, and that they their bodies are the temple of God, and that people are best advised and will live longer and godlier lives should they abstain from flesh foods, tobacco, alcohol, and caffeine. Adventists, I may also point out, do not believe in hell—that is, they don't believe that hell exists, not yet, and that when it does it will function as a cleansing fire, wiping away sinners forever, each body burning according to the extent of his or her own evil.

I might then explain that the Seventh-day Adventists were co-founded by a young prophetess named Ellen G. White, who, at the age of nine, had been walking home from school with her twin sister. A classmate shouted her name. Young Ellen turned around, this classmate hurled—apparently for no other reason than meanness—a rock, which struck the prophetess-to-be squarely in the nose. Ellen spent the next three weeks unconscious. Though she would recover, she would remain ill for years and battle various health problems for the remainder of her life. At nineteen, however, she experienced the first of what would henceforth be many visions, which included a tour of heaven where she witnessed saints receiving their crowns, each of whom were pleased with whatever amount of jewels had been set within.

There are some things, however, that I tend not to mention, things that the average Adventist would probably also keep under wraps, at least while delivering an initial introduction to the church, because these facts—taken out of their historical context, or situated outside the timetable of biblical prophecy, as it is understood by Adventists—might lead outsiders to dismiss fundamental beliefs before they've had time to digest how church founders arrived at their conclusions. For instance, I've never told my students that Ellen G. White's first book, called "An Appeal to Mothers," catalogues the myriad evils and diseases—including "disobedience," "looks of depravity," "manifestations of ingratitude," "impatience under restraint," "morose tempers excited to jealousy," "blindness," "epilepsy," "deformity," "ill-health," "diabetes," and even "death"—that would likely result from the practice of "solitary vice," a phrase that, were I to use it in class, I would no doubt need to explain was better known in our modern era as "masturbation." I would probably not explain how many Adventists believe that, in the End of Time, the Mark of the Beast would be given to those who worship on Sunday, or that those who worship on Sunday—even now—were inadvertently bringing honor to Satan. I have never—not once, in all my years of explaining Adventism to students via these mini-lectures—included the Adventist notion that each person has a recording angel in heaven, and that a person's every deed has been committed to heavenly parchment, and that someday Jesus Christ will read this book and blot out only the sins that you have specifically asked Him to forgive, and that Adventists believe He is—even as I type this—ministering in the Most Holy Place of the Heavenly Sanctuary.

I'm willing to bet if you're an Adventist, and you're reading this now, assuming you've gotten this far, you're thinking, *He's getting it wrong.* And to a certain extent I probably am. Because I know how difficult—if not impossible—it is to say "all Adventists believe," or "all Adventists do x, y, or z." Adventists are people, and as such, they are, as individuals, defined by their differences as much as by their similarities, no different from the members of any other religion. I have known Adventists who drink coffee and those who do not; Adventists who eat meat and those who do not; Adventists who abide by the dietary restrictions in Leviticus and those who welcome a lobster dinner or pepperoni on their pizza; Adventists who drink wine and Adventists who wouldn't take so much as a sip; Adventists who go to the movies and those who have never once stepped foot in a theater (for Sister White had warned that no Christian would want to be caught there during the Second Coming); Adventists who watch television on Sabbath, who will eat at restaurants on Sabbath, and those who, like the husband of the sister of an ex-girlfriend of mine, filled up their gas tanks in secret on Saturday, for fear that their parents would find out they'd purchased fuel on the seventh day. I have known Adventists who profess a deep and abiding love for the works of Ellen White and those who couldn't care less, as well as at least one Adventist who does not believe in God at all, but who simply loves Adventist culture and its traditions. I know lapsed Adventists—like the man who was a former president of his Adventist college's senior class, and then spent decades driving a Greyhound bus from L.A. to Las Vegas, where he lost hundreds of thousands of dollars—who believe Adventism is the truth but that living the Adventist life is simply too difficult, that the spirit might be willing but the flesh is weak, and therefore they know, even as they tip back shots of whiskey and light cigarettes, that they are doomed. I know Adventists who throw balls on Sabbath, who won't swim (though wading is okay), who won't indulge in the playing of any games whatsoever, except those that reveal the extent of their players' knowledge of biblical trivia. I know Adventists who curse and blaspheme and those who frown upon the use of "gosh" or "gee." I know Adventists who won't put up Christmas trees or celebrate Halloween or Easter because, they say, these holidays have pagan origins, and that those who participate in their celebration are honoring, albeit inadvertently, the devil. I know Adventists who support gay marriage and women's ordination, and those who vehemently oppose both, Adventists with tattoos and piercings and those who won't wear so much as a wedding ring, or even a friendship bracelet, for fear that said adornment would draw undue attention to their physical bodies, or make them look "worldly," or that they were concerned with the fleeting and superficial realm of contemporary fashion. I knew those who dressed themselves in brand name clothes and those who—though not shabby—dressed plainly and conservatively; Adventists who blended in and those who embodied the teaching of 1 Peter 2:9, wherein the author, believed to be writing to the persecuted churches of Asia Minor, declared that his audience was "a chosen generation, a royal priesthood, an holy nation, a peculiar people" and that they should "shew forth the praises of him" who hath called them "out of darkness" and "into his marvelous light."

As fun as it sometimes is to observe the dumbfounded reactions I get whenever I catalog the peculiarities of Adventism, I also can't help but feel a little sheepish. It's partly because Adventism isn't *all* weird. And it's partly because there's no efficient way of summing it up. I know when I'm giving this little intro that I'm just scraping the surface. I'm not telling the whole story. Then again, no description I provide ends up feeling accurate enough to be true.

What is absolutely, positively true, though? I loved growing up Adventist. I loved singing "Onward Christian Soldiers" and "This Little Light of Mine" and "Only a Boy Named David." I loved clapping my hands together to mime "shoot the artillery" and shielding my candle finger so Satan couldn't blow it out and swinging my imaginary slingshot 'round and 'round before the stone hit Goliath in the forehead and "the giant came tumbling down." I loved eating

Worthington meat substitutes like Big Franks and Fri Chik. More than anything else, I loved my Adventist family—grandparents, great grandparents, cousins, uncles, and aunts. And most of all, I loved my Adventist parents.

I might've sometimes wished my parents would "lighten up"—that they would let me stay up later, eat more dessert, watch more TV—but I never once thought that any other parents were better than my own. I never once in all my years of living with them saw them fight. Never heard them argue. Never eavesdropped on a "heated conversation." Never witnessed them raise their voices in anger or frustration at the other. Whatever conflicts or arguments my parents had, if any, they kept between themselves. I never knew why, but I assume now that it's because they feared that somehow their children would be hurt or damaged by witnessing their parents do anything but treat one another with love and respect.

And this bothered me.

I knew other kids who had Adventist parents who could seem "cooler" than mine, but the shortcomings of these parents were obvious and, in the end, overshadowed whatever permissive tendencies I wished my own parents would emulate. One of my friend's dads sang along to Ray Stevens songs and listened to Michael Jackson and took my friend to see *Ghostbusters* at the local Twin Cinema, but he also left his wife not long after she'd been diagnosed with MS and took up with another woman, who I remember as being charmingly foul-mouthed but strangely and obviously less-attractive. Another friend's dad kept a stack of *Playboy* magazines in the closet of his guest bedroom; I know because my sister found them during a game of hide and seek. It seemed like a good number of my friends' parents were divorced, or were getting divorced, and even if the couple was still together, they were still far less appealing to me than my own parents, maybe because they were less funny, or were a little too pushy, or were unafraid of reprimanding kids who weren't their own. How come everybody else had parents who were obviously flawed, who had hang-ups, who acted selfishly, who occasionally said and did ugly things? Why couldn't I have parents like these, parents who said and did ugly things? Was it too much to ask, even, that they do just *one* ugly thing? I didn't want them to be monsters; I just wanted them to be more human, because then I'd have less to live up to. Because when I measured myself against my parents, the distance between who I was and the kinds of people they were seemed insurmountable.

That's not to say I couldn't find little ways to resent them, like when my dad wanted me to help him retrieve sticks of kindling from the lumberyard, or drive out to the Land to cut wood with a motorized splitter whose hydraulic arm lowered its blade and crunched through the heart of a log like a guillotine in slow-mo. Or when my mother forced my sister and me to turn off the TV and sweep the porch or clean our rooms or go outside to play with our golden retrievers, which our mother always referred to as "those dogs," reminding us that we were the ones who had wanted them, we had promised to love them and take care of them, and of course we had every intention of doing so, but that was before they grew up, before their fur—because they were outside dogs—got matted, and before my dog, the fat, dumb one, gave up retrieving altogether because his sister always beat him to thrown balls and so during fetch time simply let her do the retrieving while he turned over to receive a belly rub from the bottom of my tennis shoe because I couldn't bear to touch his dirty underside with a bare hand.

The question of how I "got out of" or "left" the denomination seems to be one that I am most often called upon to answer, and I don't know that I have ever told the truth to anybody who's ever asked it, and that includes myself. When searching for an answer to this questions, my brain, which has been conditioned to prefer the concrete and think of time as a linear progression, automatically attempts to scroll backwards, so as to assign significance to a particular moment in time, perhaps one in which I came to some realization or experienced an epiphany. Like most humans, I imagine, I have had my share of those, and I can think now of my second semester of college, when, living in my first time in an apartment, a place where neither parent nor teacher nor resident assistant nor dean could record my comings and goings, and so for the first time in my life, I could choose whether or not I wanted to go to church and would face no immediate consequence—no parental punishment, no mark against an attendance record— and so for the first time in my life I chose not to go. Perhaps it could be said that this was the kind of moment that I consider when attempting to find an answer to the question: "When did you stop being an Adventist?" Even so, such a question seems to fail to consider the notion that a person like me—a person who was raised in the middle of nowhere, in the melancholic hollows of the mountains of Western North Carolina, in a loving and nurturing family co-captained by two parents who had also grown up in the church, attended church schools, read church books, sang church songs, listened to church music, and church story and ate Seventh-day Adventist food—could ever really leave the Seventh-day Adventist church, or that the idea of "leaving" was any more possible than changing who my parents were, that Seventh-day Adventism was as much part of who I was as any other essential element that made me who I was, and would forever influence who I would become.

On January 19, 2020, I decided to go see the lights. The air in the cove at my father's house was crisp and bracing. Streams roared. The sky had cleared itself of clouds. After the sun had gone down and the stars had come out, my father turned out all the lights in the house. We stood in his bedroom. Stared out the windows. I can't remember how much time passed. For a long time, we didn't see anything.

"There's one," my dad finally said.

"Where?"

"Over there," he replied, pointing. "Down toward the left."

I didn't see anything.

"There's another one," he said.

Missed that one too. And the next. And the next. I thought maybe he was making them up. Or maybe his eyes—thanks to his glasses—were better than mine. Eventually, I thought I'd spotted something in my peripheral vision, which, according to my father, was where they often appeared. I was skeptical. After all, when I closed my eyes and stared into the dark, it was never dark for long: shapes would eventually begin to form and images would fade in and out, emerging and merging and submerging again; was a similar phenomenon happening now?

"They're not very active tonight," my father said. We said goodnight and I retired to my room, where I watched the slow fade of hundreds of glow-in-the-dark stars I'd stickered to the walls and ceilings two decades before. At 3 a.m., my phone rang and woke me. The screen said, *Dad.* I answered.

"They're going again," he said. I made my way downstairs. I stood at the window. Again, I thought I'd seen something, but wasn't sure, and said so, wondering aloud whether or not I had convinced myself that I'd somehow made up what I thought I'd seen, simply because I'd wanted to see *something.*

"Think about how long we stood here tonight," Dad said. "And how for the longest time we never saw anything. So, if you think you saw something, you probably did."

I couldn't argue with that. Or maybe I just didn't know how. I kind of didn't care. It was enough to stand there, next to my father, staring through those windows, into the night. It was the first time I could ever remember being in his presence for such a sustained period, experiencing something that neither of us understood, and for which we had no words to explain.

III. FASCINATING PHENOMENA

Unmoored: "to be free of moorings."

Moorings: the various cables and ropes that attach to a ship to hold it in place upon the water.

The more I thought about it, the more I had to acknowledge that this was the way I felt. Moreover, it was the way I wanted to feel. I wanted to travel backward through time, if only in my mind, back to a place where my mother had been her "normal" self, to a time before she'd been sick, and imagine—or at least relish the wish—that I might tell her that I was sorry about what would happen to her.

But also? I did not want to feel unmoored. The more time I spent on earth, the more memories I made, and the more I had to keep track of and organize. Only I couldn't do it. Trying to remember some years, like 2013, say, or 2014, summoned nothing in particular. Others, like 2015, the year that Kelly had been diagnosed with ductal carcinoma in situ and had opted to undergo a double mastectomy with reconstruction, a process that involved months of recovery, during which my youngest cousin, the son of my favorite aunt, had died in his bedroom at his parents' house of what had first appeared to be an overdose of heroin but was later determined to be pure fentanyl, had been seared into my brain. The big events I remembered. But the in-betweens? Not so much.

But what I couldn't forget? My mother. Had any grandmother in the history of the world delighted more in the birth of her first grandchild? I doubted it. She and my father made frequent visits, during Elijah's first years on earth, to Lafayette, Indiana, where Kelly was matriculating through her rhetoric PhD program, and where I worked as an instructor of English. She never went anywhere without her digital camera, and shot thousands of photos of her cherubic grandchild, many of which she printed and cut out and glued to cardboard booklets she made for her grandson, each page adorned with stickers of flowers and birds and animals, captioned with little bits of narrative. In short, she showered him—as she had me and my sister—with unabashed, unconditional love.

My mother never pressured me to return to her beloved church. She never condemned my decision to leave, though no doubt she silently questioned it. Sometimes, when I was home, and I had to pass through my parents' bedroom to retrieve something from their bathroom—fingernail clippers, an extra toothbrush, a razor—I'd glance down at my mother's bedroom table and note the books stacked there. For years, it seemed, there was always one on top: *The Power of Praying for Your Adult Children*. But she never proselytized. She might, on a CD she'd recorded for Elijah, include an Adventist hymn or story. Even when she called one day, because she happened to be serving as the church secretary and was updating the directory, and asked if I still wanted to keep my name on "the books," and I told her that, actually, it might be a good idea to remove it, she didn't put up a fight. Didn't try to win me over with an argument. Which somehow kind of made me feel worse. Like she was hoping her quiet example and unconditional affection would do the trick, and all the years of unselfishly loving me to an inch of my life would be the exact investment required for me to amend my ways and return home.

In the evenings that winter, I often donned headphones and scrolled past photos I had taken of the photographs from albums that my mother had so diligently assembled, as if she had known, unconsciously, perhaps, that we would need to depend upon these to help us remember once she was gone. I'd pause, on the rare occasions that I found myself looking at a picture of Mom—after all, she had been the one, 99 times out of 100, to act as photographer. It was strange to acknowledge, now, her ghostlike presence in these images, as she had been there, at whatever scene said photos displayed, whether it be snow days, first days of school where my sister and I stood on our front porch steps clutching our new lunch boxes, or the glee of Christmas present opening. This combination of evening cocktail plus sad piano music and photographs of my mother's photographs had the effect of creating a rift in time.

There's been some development with the lights.

My father texted this sentence on January 27, 2020: the day after Kobe Bryant, his daughter, and their friends perished when their helicopter crashed. Earlier that morning, I'd watched an online video that purported to have recorded the sound of the chopper slamming into the side of a fog-shrouded mountain, turning passengers into what I imagined was now a slush of still-hot embers.

"Siri," I said. "Call Dad."

"Calling Dad," Siri said.

The phone rang.

"Hello?" he said.

"What's changed?"

"A lot," he said. "Last night, I woke up at 3 a.m. Or maybe quarter of 2. There was no moon. Actually, it was the dark of the moon. So everything was dark. Pitch black. I didn't see any of the regular flashing lights. But then I saw something different. A swath of light where you go to walk across the creek to reach the pond. A ray of light lighting up the trees. I put my glasses on, and must have fallen asleep. I woke up wearing them. This morning, at 4:30, I looked out again. No question. It was a beam of light. Then, at 6 o'clock, it appeared again. For about thirty seconds. Then it went out. This *big* light was larger than the beam of a car's headlights, and it came down the other ridge above the pond. I don't know what to say except it had the qualities of a beam of light. Like in the summertime when the moon comes up and there's a hole in the trees where the light comes through."

"Were you wearing your glasses?"

"Of course I was wearing my glasses."

"Okay. Keep going."

"If you had a big truck with lights on the roof, it was like that. A big powerful light shining down. And it was going more *across* the pond than *on* the pond. And it was like when the whole column moved it pivoted from where its origin part was. A whole column of light. This morning at 5:45, it did the same thing. And when this big light appeared, so did the other lights. And in fact the big light appeared to *excite* the smaller ones. Lots of lights: white, red, yellowish. I tried to film it. But the minute I touched my phone, they disappeared."

"No way," I said.

"Yeah."

"What do you mean by *excited*, though?"

"I don't know. They all just seemed to be blinking faster and at regular intervals. As though they were happy to see the bigger light appear."

In my mind, I imagined the lesser lights were somehow welcoming the larger one. Like all that extra blinking. I don't know. I imagined that it might have functioned like some kind of applause.

In November of 1915, *Poetry* magazine published Wallace Stevens's poem, "Sunday Morning," which included the lines: "Death is the mother of beauty, hence from her, / Alone, shall come fulfilment to our dreams / And our desires." The first time I read this, I hadn't known what to make of that phrase. Death is the mother of beauty. I was twenty-five years old and studying English and creative writing in grad school. I'd never known what to make of most poems when I first began to read, with any seriousness or intensity, this thing we call "literature." If my memory served me correctly, the line was supposed to suggest that beauty, like life, was fleeting. Like, part of the reason that humans considered flowers beautiful had everything to do with the impermanence of their blooms. Though the phrase made sense to me now, more than ever, I'd found myself switching it around so that it read, at least in my head, "beauty is the mother of death." And in the college town where I lived, on a verdant plateau in the Appalachians, beauty was unabashedly rampant. Bluebirds on fence posts. Horses, heads jacketed with netting, swishing their tails. Begonias in pots hanging from downtown lampposts. Little gushing streams made brief appearances before disappearing into underground tunnels. Rain droplets hung gemlike from baby leaves. And every time the natural world made itself known, every single time, I'd spy a bloom or a bird or a leaf or a cloud—literally any one would do—and I'd think: Mom. And when I imagined magical lights flashing like winter fireflies in the woods she loved so much, I thought of her too.

On a web site titled "Unexplained Mysteries," a user named Dene, who qualified his moniker with the phrase "Alien Embryo," posted a story about seeing bright flashing lights in a remote cabin in northern Wisconsin. Among the users who responded to this thread, a person named Gwynbleidd, which translates from the Welsh—or from the Elvish of the video game *The Witcher*—into "white wolf," offered a source for what he referred to as "light anomalies": the International Earthlight Alliance. Sounded like something I needed to check out.

The International Earthlight Alliance—"a non-profit organization inspiring interest in science through stringent high-tech investigation of anomalies"—doesn't believe in ghosts, either. As an organization committed to science, it ruled out the idea that unexplained lights could—or should—be classified as "paranormal."

"People who have had close encounters with the lights often report unusual sensations," a page on the IAE's website claims, "which they have interpreted as mystical or even religious experiences. This may be due to an explainable phenomenon—human encounter with strong time-varying magnetic fields. Preliminary measurements indicate strong magnetic activity in the vicinity of Earthlights. Canadian neurophysiologist Michael Persinger has demonstrated in the laboratory that he can create 'religious,' or subjectively 'paranormal' experiences in volunteers wearing a helmet that induces such magnetic fields in their brains."

It's not that the International Earthlight Alliance has anything against ghosts, per se. They just think that the stories we humans tell about them should be investigated, rather than simply denied. The same goes with mysterious lights.

Lights of unknown origin have appeared since the dawn of recorded history. For this reason and many others, the IEA invites members of the public to become "Earthlight scouts."

According to the IEA website, the majority of scientists, as it turns out, care very little about mysterious, otherworldly lights. "Historically," the IEA says, "science has been a difficult profession. Creative individuals who have made the greatest discoveries have often been ostracized, persecuted, and even imprisoned by their peers." Take Galileo, for instance, whose telescope was once referred to as an "instrument of the devil." Or Giordano Bruno, who proposed that stars were distant suns orbited by their own planets, a supposition that led to the idea that perhaps other life might exist in the far reaches of the universe, that the universe was infinite, and that it might have no center. For the promotion of such ideas, Bruno was burned at the stake.

The IEA also claims that, in the present day, science's "publish or peril" model encourages researchers to focus on activities that will ensure future funding, often at the expense of work that is creative in nature. This focus on funding, according to the IEA, rather than on "ideas," contributed to a negative "science culture." Overly competitive, science has become prone to politics, and funding favoritism. Established scientists invested in their own ideas are often hostile to new ideas and creative solutions that challenge the status quo. Since there's not financial incentive by profiting off the lights, and since to my knowledge, mysterious lights weren't making people sick either, then there also isn't much of a cultural incentive to investigate the lights.

And so, mysterious lights continue to appear all over the earth and nobody knows why. Scientists don't care about them enough to find out. And they don't seem to care that Earthlight Scouts, or the people who see them, tell stories about what they have seen.

"Get this," Dad said. "*Last* night, I woke up in the middle of the night, about three or so, and looked out to see the lights."

"Oh yeah? See anything?"

"You know the hickory tree? The one just outside my window?"

"Of course," I said. I had no idea which one he was talking about.

"Last night," he said, "when I woke up in the middle of the night, the whole tree was illuminated. It was almost like the lights were under the tree. I couldn't be sure which way the light was coming. But it appeared that the entire tree was lit. And then I looked up and saw that the tree was full of bright green leaves."

"Leaves?"

"Yes," he said. "Shiny and green. I rubbed my eyes and looked, thinking maybe I was making it all up. But no. There they were. Thick as summer. I tried to take a picture. But as soon as I touched my phone, the light went out. And the leaves disappeared."

"And you're sure you weren't dreaming?"

"Of course," he said.

"Wow," I said. I wrote this down in the little book. I could see the leaves in my mind, could imagine the ghostly glow. I couldn't help but be jealous.

I typed "flashing lights in woods" into a search engine. The phrase returned a handful of hits: a Reddit thread about aliens, a phrase highlighted from a true crime book called *Hunting Justice*, and a Yahoo thread attempting to identify the source of a light flashing in a forest, which a user named Lolita Hayes answered by saying, "It's either fairies (like the ones in kids' books), gnomes, Wood Elves (I like that one), swamp gas, ancient warriors and orcs in the water, My Precious, Mr. Burns from the *X-files/Simpsons* episode (when he's tripping and radioactive) or maybe (this is the scariest) militia guys doing training runs for Armageddon! Lock your doors!"

I entered "flashing lights in woods" again—this time leaving out the quotation marks—and was rewarded with seven million plus hits. I learned that lights whose source could not be identified had gone by many names. Corpse candles. Flying flame. Foo fighters. Ghost beacons. Night suns. Spook lights. Spirit lanterns. Unctuous vapors. I stumbled upon a Reddit post where users shared their experiences of having witnessed mysterious, blinking lights in the woods. Most of these witnesses had been, like my father, in remote locations. I read about firefly flash patterns. I read about foxfire—the bioluminescent fungi that appears in decaying wood. I read about the will-o'-the-wisp, a legendary ghost light from folklore whose Wikipedia page informed me that "In literature, will-o'-the-wisp metaphorically refers to a hope or goal that leads one on but is impossible to reach, or something one finds sinister and confounding." Thanks to a site called "Occult World," I learned that "Ghost lights have the power to fascinate, and some individuals who see them do not want the mystique spoiled by an explanation." That made sense to me. But I supposed my father would find this a less appealing perspective. He had never struck me as the kind of man who embraced uncertainty. Or ambiguity. For most of life's troubles and trials, he had answers. God, our loving heavenly father, who longed to be reunited with his creation, was in control. Satan, his enemy, roved the earth like a lion, seeking those he might devour, and in the meantime sought to sully the reputation of the Most High. Jesus, the son—the sacrifice—was the solution. And he was coming back to save us—at least, those of us who believed in and loved him, and proved that we did by following his rules. It was a narrative whose storyline nothing could complicate: not disease, not uncertainty, and certainly not death.

I entered the phrase "ghost lights" into Amazon and clicked on "books." The first hit that came up? *North Carolina Ghost Lights and Legends* by Charles Gritzner.

Wow, I thought. *On point.*

South Dakota State University's Department of Geography website had an email for Charles "Fritz" Gritzner that was defunct, but thanks to a connection at his publishing company, Carolina Wren Press, I was given his personal email address with a promise that Gritzner was "a delight."

I wrote him a letter.

Hi Dr. Gritzner,

I am an Associate Professor of Creative Writing who just ordered North Carolina Ghost Lights and Legends. *I'm working on a book of my own, a memoir about, among other things, the influence of Seventh-day Adventism on my rearing, and the death of my mother at a relatively early age (from Alzheimer's). My father lives in a remote part of southwestern North Carolina, on land that borders national forest. Since December, he has seen flashing lights in the woods surrounding his house. They're brief, very fast flashes of very bright light; I know because I've seen them, too, as have many other visitors. My father has also seen a kind of slow-moving band of light that seems to hover over the ground. Once, a light lit up a hickory tree outside his bedroom window and when he looked up into its branches, he could see green leaves–in early February. This is all very strange and I wonder if you've heard stories like this before. I know the answer to this is probably in your book but if you ever had the time or the interest I would be very interested to speak with you about this matter.*

Sincerely,

MV

One of the very first stories I wrote–a copy of which I recently found in my garage, on mildewed pages printed with dot matrix letters–was a first-person account of a boy who was obsessed by the idea that his parents might actually be "alien robots." At the top of the first page, under my name, the phrase USE FOR FICTION appeared in all caps, a designation I'd made—I now assumed—for the benefit of the creative writing course I'd been taking. And while the story had indeed been fictional, the main conceit—a child's speculations concerning his parents' true identities—hadn't been. I'd made that part up years before, back when I'd been a kid negotiating the remote wilderness of southwestern North Carolina, and when I'd spent a good portion of my playtime imagining alternatives to my own reality. One particular scenario I often entertained was that my parents might not actually be my real parents; they might instead be aliens in disguise, or robots, or both. I can't remember when the idea had first occurred to me, though I do remember wondering, on the occasions when I followed my father through the woods, attempting to shield myself from getting slapped in the face by the rhododendron limbs he allowed to slingshot toward me as he plowed through underbrush, if he was, in fact, my actual father. I would acknowledge our unthinkable distance from the house, and how far we were from anything resembling civilization, and I would wonder whether this man might be leading me, as Abraham had led Isaac so long ago, into the wilderness to sacrifice me. In order for this fantasy to be viable—and I suppose it was a kind of fantasy, a kind of fiction I wrote in my head in order to scare myself—I had to imagine that my father was someone other than he appeared to be, and that the man I'd always known represented a kind of fiction.

The truth was, though, that if there was something truly robotic about my parents, it was that they were utterly predictable: you always could depend upon them to effortlessly conform to whatever their church and families and friends asked or needed them to be. And so, their ways of going about in the world were, in some sense, alien to me:

a kid who was not naturally disposed to reading his bible or putting others before himself. I suppose it had been comforting for me to imagine, then, that my parents—who I'd never seen argue or fight or even raise their voices at one another—hadn't really been human. It was easier to imagine that they were simply aliens. Or maybe even machines.

Dear Professor Vollmer:

Your book sounds fascinating, although your mother's death must be a very difficult subject to discuss. Life takes strange and often very sad turns. Good luck with the project!

Where, specifically (in as much detail as possible), do the lights appear that you and your father have seen? As a geographer, I begin with location and go from there.

The lights that you describe are quite common and to my knowledge (and I have studied the phenomenon for at least three decades) remain unexplained (other than those that are the lights of vehicles at a distance).

For example, from Thomas Divide Overlook on the Blue Ridge Parkway north of Cherokee, I saw an absolutely amazing and totally inexplicable white light that moved some distance (a couple of miles?) in a very straight line and above the treetops. It then stopped and remained illuminated for the hour I stayed at the overlook. Additionally, the first light discussed in "The West," Big Laurel, was described as being a mistake—one that I placed as possibly being confused with lights seen near Big Laurel, Kentucky. Subsequently, I met a gentleman who lives near the small settlement of Big Laurel (Madison County, North Carolina) and claims to have seen lights wandering through the woods on numerous occasions.

Again, thank you so much for writing and sharing your

experience and other information. Please be back in touch once you know the kinds of information I need to include the light in the second edition of my book. I look forward to hearing from you again.

Warm regards,

Fritz
Charles F. Gritzner
Distinguished Professor Emeritus of Geography
South Dakota State University

I used to think that *machine* had been an apt word to describe my mother, not only because she'd possessed such inexhaustible reserves of energy, but also because she'd accepted so completely—and without the slightest reservation—the program that had been encoded into the mainframe of her brain: the one that told her how best to behave. I rarely saw her make a mistake. Never heard her complain. Then again, she didn't have room in her schedule for the kind of sustained reflection that gives birth to critique. Nearly everything she did—cook, clean, play piano, sew, manage my father's dental office, carpool, run volunteer programs—she did for the benefit of someone else.

As far as I could tell, my mother had been gifted with an impeccable internal barometer, one that allowed her to identify, without fail, bad from good and right from wrong: I never once saw her struggle with a moral quandary, never witnessed an occasion when she seemed confused about so-called "spiritual" matters. Though she was observant and knowledgeable about the natural world—pointing out jack-in-the-pulpits and red-winged blackbirds and "hearts-a-bustin'"—she was not overly introspective. Rarely gave the impression that she was anxious or that there was ever anything about living her life she worried *that* much about. I suspect that the narrative she'd received concerning the Adventist story regarding the origins and fate of the universe in which she lived had always made perfect sense, and that she'd always viewed human history, from the time she was old enough to understand such a thing, as a constant struggle between Jesus Christ and his adversary, Satan, and that her church had always been the one that provided the truest and most accurate picture of the character of God. Whether she could articulate with any confidence the specifics concerning what the members of other churches believed, I can't say, as to my knowledge she'd made no substantial investigations into the particulars of other religions. Then again, why would she need to, when the truths of her own denomination were clearly so self-evident?

So yes. The word *machine* once seemed like an appropriate word to describe her.

Until it wasn't.

Because here's the thing: machines do not forget. Machines do not lose their keys. Their purses and pills. Machines do not try to use the un-pronged end of a fork to eat their mashed potatoes. Or try to shave their armpits with a shower squeegee. Machines do not forget the names of their loved ones.

Machines do not study recipes for hummingbird food (*1 cup sugar, 4 cups water, boil water, add sugar, stir, let cool*) and, because they find these instructions impossible to decipher, say, "I can't do anything anymore." Machines do not cry. Machines do not need to be told, "It's okay," and "I'm here to help." Machines do not need to be comforted by hugs. Which means that my mother, at some point, stopped being a machine and became something else: a person who, when my father pulled up an old photo of her and my sister that I'd posted to Instagram, said, "Who's that?"

Hello Fritz,

I have been steadfastly recording my father's experience with the lights and am attaching a brief video that show a few. You can get a great view of this property on Google Earth. I don't know how clear it will be to see but obviously the area is densely wooded and mountainous. The house sits atop a steep, grassy hill. Two streams come together at the bottom of the hill and there's a pipe in the stream on the right that feeds a pond at the bottom of the hill and across the driveway. Across the stream on the left, there's a big grassy field which was once, before it had been cleared, a kind of swampy rhododendron thicket. Two old logging roads (one of which is severely overgrown) lead on either side of the house up the mountain. If you follow the road on the right side (if you're looking down at the house from the Google Earth view), you will come to our family cemetery.

As you can see in the video, the lights exist as very fast flashes. I've only witnessed a few myself and they were just as seen in the video. They appear to be coming from the woods. They don't appear in the sky and are often seen from a distance of a few hundred yards, though my father has seen them closer to the house as well. The lights are normally white in color but other colors (red, blue, yellow) have also been observed. No one to my knowledge has stayed up the entire night to watch them, but they don't seem to prefer a particular time (save for darkness).

My father has seen these lights nearly every night since he first noticed them, aside from a three day stretch when the moon was near its fullest and ground covered in snow. Sometimes they are more active than others, sometimes continuous (one every couple seconds), rare for a minute to go by without seeing one. These flashing lights generally do not move, though dad did say one night he saw one swoosh upward. Sometimes the lights are brighter, and sometimes they appear more frequently than other nights.

My father has also reported a band of light (reportedly about the brightness of moonlight during a full moon) that moves parallel to the road between his house and the house where my grandmother used to live, about a quarter mile away. As I said before, one night my father awoke on three different occasions to see a hickory tree outside his bedroom window illuminated by this "big light" as he calls it and the tree itself appeared to be full of green leaves.

My father has been living in this cove for nearly thirty years and has never seen anything like this. He remembers going to see the lights on Brown Mountain when he was a teenager. He would be very interested in speaking with you, as would I. I had a long conversation with him last night. Whenever I talk about the lights to people, they tend to automatically think that my mother is communicating from beyond the grave. This is not my father's point of view though.

Thanks for reading and for all your help. Please feel free to ask any questions. Also, if there might be a time in the near future when I could talk to you on the phone, that would be great.

Best,
MV

A site titled "Tree Spirit Wisdom" assured me that having a special encounter with a hickory tree meant that "the tree is asking us to release something we have been holding onto that now holds us" and that "This is a time of finding the right balance between having fun and having a safety net. If we feel like we carry the weight of the world on our shoulders now is the time to unburden ourselves so we can become rejuvenated. We must honor the wisdom of releasing and see this as a new beginning. Be gentle with yourself and others during these times of shedding.'"

I texted this paragraph to my father. And despite the fact that I could see that it had both been delivered and read, he never acknowledged its reception. And why would he? The phrase "Tree Spirit Wisdom" had a decidedly New Age connotation. Which meant, I supposed, it resonated with danger.

Howdy, Matt:

What a fascinating phenomenon you report! Absolutely amazing! And based upon your experiences (numerous sightings) I am absolutely positive that you have a "legitimate" ghost light. I can't think of anything natural/normal that would explain what you describe.

When did your father first see the lights? Do other people living in the general area see lights (in other words, is the phenomenon rather widespread)? You indicate that most of them are stationary, or relatively so. This certainly rules out vehicle lights in the distance as seen through the trees.

There are several locations in the state from which similar light displays have been described, e.g., see the two references to lights near Cullowhee and my sighting north of Cherokee (Thomas Divide Overlook).

I will retain this information and hope that the book goes into a second printing, in which case I can make changes/ additions. Assuming this occurs, I'll be back in touch with you. And, of course, if I have the good fortune of being in the area again, I would love to drop by and take a look at the lights myself.

Thank you again for being in touch and sharing this fascinating information.

Warm regards,

Fritz

That was the last time I heard from Fritz. I'm not sure what more he might've needed from me, or I him. I read the pertinent passages from his book, which I found intriguing, especially the final section. In the end, Gritzner, who provides tantalizing descriptions of notorious lights and the folklore that they have inspired, doesn't determine the origins of the various phenomenon he investigates, but he does arrive at an important conclusion: that ghost lights are worthy of scientific study.

It is a shame that so little serious attention has been directed—particularly by scientists—toward gaining a better understanding of these fascinating phenomena. The same holds true for the body of folktales that has evolved over time in association with the lights. I find it extremely surprising that ghost light-related legends have scarcely been touched by folklorists in North Carolina or elsewhere.

From Gritzner's perspective, there was "no need to turn

to the supernatural in search of answers." The key, in the end, was for people to start paying attention. For some reason, this made me think—once again—of my mother. Was there anyone I'd ever known who paid attention to the world like she had? Once upon a time, she could see the shape of a leaf on a tree and summon its name. She pried rocks from the creek and arranged them into borders for her flowerbeds. She kept records of birds who visited her feeders. I couldn't help but wish she were still here. With her wits about her. To observe and record the lights. But then again, maybe if she were here, the lights wouldn't be.

IV. BEARING WITNESS

There were, in the spring of 2020, two men named Evan associated with the Master of Fine Arts program at Virginia Tech: one was a professor, the other a student. Both were my friends. Evan the professor, a white man from New Mexico, was older—in his early forties—but significantly smaller in physical stature than Evan the student, a Black man from Virginia who'd recently turned thirty. Even so, the smaller but older Evan was known as Big Evan, while the younger but more decidedly muscular Evan was known as Lil Evan.

I hadn't known what to make of Lil Evan when I first met him. He could be deeply attentive in class, nodding and mm-ing affirmatively, contributing to discussions and participating in brainstorms and close readings of the texts we read. But he could also be quiet and distant, as if even though he was only sitting across the table he was far, far away. He had studied philosophy as an undergraduate at Ole Miss, a university he'd attended, in part, because he wanted to pay his respects to the Deep South. Before that, he'd served in Afghanistan: a nine-month deployment, the specifics of which he had been recording and shaping in the stories he was working on. He often sent me works-in-progress. He'd played basketball and football and soccer as a young man. He'd introduced me to oxtail at a Caribbean restaurant in Roanoke. He loved outer space. And nature. And birds. He'd dated girls on Facebook without ever seeing them in person.

I asked Lil Evan if he wanted to take a trip to my dad's house. We could hike. Relax for a couple days. Investigate the lights.

"Absolutely," Evan said. "When?"

On February 23, 2020, Lil Evan and I drove to my dad's house.

My dad wasn't there; he'd gone to Chicago to attend the largest annual gathering of dentists in America, where he would no doubt wander vast showrooms of new and improved dental smocks and cavity-fighting technology. That was another reason to go: I wanted to see—and I'm not sure why this was important—if the lights might appear in his absence.

They say you can't go home again. Don't tell that to my brain. Its limbic system frequently conspires to return me, often against my own will, to the little house where I grew up, in that cove at the bottom of a mountain—the one my parents decided to sell so that they could move into the bigger house up at the Land. I've been doing it for as long as I can remember; it's now no longer something I can control. Head does what head wants to do. Head reads, for instance, a story in which a house appears and if said house has not been precisely described, head automatically places the story's characters inside that little house. It's like, really, head? That's all you got? You don't have to make up a house from wholesale cloth or anything, but come on. The same one? *Every* time? How many houses have you visited, anyway, head? Hundreds? Thousands? And *this* is the one you want? This is the one you insist on? There's nothing wrong with it, but aside from the sixteen-windowed sunporch, which, I'll grant you is pretty nice, especially because it looks out onto a rhododendron thicket, which means even in winter your view remains green, this house isn't—from an architectural point of view at least—all that special.

It was, however, the one I'd grown up in and where, until I turned fourteen and left home to attend boarding school, I'd spent more time than anywhere else on earth. I didn't even think about it; if someone started to tell a story, or I happened to read one in my *Junior Guide* magazine, a new copy of which I obtained every week at the Sabbath School service at church, or if I happened to be taking a long car ride with my family and someone inserted a *Your Story Hour* cassette into the tape deck and Aunt Sue and Uncle Dan began to weave a tale about "Little Miss Bossy" or the lost dog who found his way home or the kid who was tempted to steal some "dough" from the bank vault he was sweeping, and they neglected to say that the family lived in an igloo or hut or mansion, I took whatever characters appeared in my mind and set them inside the place I knew better than any other, and in this way, the little house where I grew up—with that glorious sunroom, its kitchen wallpapered with images of various herbs, its basement filled with old dental equipment, its attic stuffed with boxes of Christmas decorations and the clothes of long-dead relatives—became the stage upon which I set all my imaginary dramas.

My parents had populated the house with antique furniture. Almost everything they owned—despite the floral print couch and entertainment cabinet—looked like it'd been made by hand in the previous century. My parents had bought nearly all of it in at flea markets in southern California, during the first years of their marriage, when my father was in dental school and my mother was working as a hygienist. The furniture was part of the house's interior geography. And some of it, like the hall tree, was weird. The hall tree—a high-backed chair with a mirror and golden prongs upon which the family hung their coats and jackets and scarves—resembled a wooden throne, and sometimes my sister and I sat upon it and pretended we were King or Queen. The hall tree's seat, whose hinged lid tilted open, functioned as space for the storage of gloves and hats. There was a big oval mirror and a seat back that reached halfway up the wall. Beneath the mirror, there was an escutcheon with a brass tassel, a crenellated triangle that, once tugged, would open a small door in the seat back, revealing a slim space that we sometimes pretended was a mailbox. In addition to the hall tree, there was an old icebox with three doors and brass latches and a dry sink and a couple of china cabinets and dressers and a set of drawers especially for storing sheet music and another set of see-through glass drawers that contained various buttons and threads and a tall wooden trunk-like chest that housed fabrics and varieties of linens that my mother used in her sewing. In the dining room, next to a wooden cabinet, stood a butter churn, one that had actually been built to churn actual butter, a canister with a lid through which a broomstick-like wand stuck out that one could lift up and down but which my mother would rather not have me "mess with." At the top of the dish cabinet sat a glossy music box that, once its knob was twisted, unspooled a tinkling little song his parents claimed as their

own—"Claire de Lune." The song was to my ears a mani-
festation of love. Each note, each part of the song seemed
to embody and express the mystery of what it meant to
fall in love with someone and for them to love you back, a
notion that I found paralyzingly sorrowful, since the idea of
getting married and having a wife and then family of my own
struck me as so incomprehensibly far away and that it was
difficult—if not impossible—to imagine. The occasion of my
future wedding—supposing I could find a woman who liked
me as much as I liked her, which I doubted would ever be
possible—seemed eons away. It was much easier to imagine
Jesus coming and taking us all to heaven, where, as I understood it, there would be no man and woman and therefore
no new babies, which was also sad because babies were cute
and funny as long as they were happy, which, in heaven, they
certainly would be.

Town was a five-minute drive away: three stop lights, a grocery
store, a twin cinema, a post office, two-dozen churches, three
banks, a hospital, a handful of gas stations, and three facto-
ries that produced custom wood furniture, Lee jeans, and
outboard motors, respectively. There was a main street where
teenagers drove Mustangs and Chevys on Friday nights, a
parking lot where they raised hoods and revved engines.
There was a barbershop where old men told stories about
bear, coons, huckleberries, railroads, gardens, and the
dearth or surfeit of rain. There were mountains—blue ridges
rising above the town like the walls of an enormous fortress.
There were woods where you could find jack-in-the-pulpits
and lady's slippers and puffballs that, when squeezed, ejac-
ulated greenish smoke. There were snakes and wasps and

hog "wallers," secret waterfalls and caves where outlaws once hid. There were fields whose dirt, when plowed, surrendered pottery shards, musket balls, and arrowheads, the artifacts of a Cherokee civilization whose members, three centuries ago—before Andrew Jackson signed the Indian Removal Act of 1830, and before said Indians were rounded up and marched, at bayonet point, from cool, hemlock-shaded hollows to blistering Oklahoman prairies—would've outnumbered the white people living here now.

Despite the fact that I'd grown up here, whenever I biked down Main Street, I felt conspicuous. Maybe it was because I didn't really live in town but on its outskirts. Maybe it was because I knew so few townsfolk, while my dad couldn't go anywhere without someone stopping him, to give him a hard time about hardly working, thus embarking upon the kind of banter in which two people engage one another in mutual but affable disparagement. Maybe it was because my family belonged to a church whose members gathered together to worship on the seventh day of the week instead of the first—a church that viewed itself as separate from the rest of the world. Maybe it was because I didn't attend my local public elementary school; instead, I met five other kids in the parking lot of the Valley Plaza every morning to carpool to another town, to a private church school in a three-roomed, A-framed house. Although I was proud to say the name of my hometown—Andrews, North Carolina—I often felt like a stranger when I visited.

Evan and I stopped in town to grab supplies at Ingles grocery—marshmallows, graham crackers, chocolate, hot dogs, and potatoes, onions, and peppers for hash we intended to bake in pockets of foil nestled inside the coals of a fire—and ran into a woman who worked as a receptionist at my father's office.

"We're here to check out the lights," I said. "Assuming they show up."

"Oh Lord," she replied. "Those lights. They've got your dad agitated."

"How so?" I said.

"I don't know how else to say it. Just *agitated*."

The woman pointed to an example: the day after my father had seen the green leaves appear in the hickory tree. That day, my father had not seemed like himself. He hadn't joked or poked fun at his employees. In between patients, he stared into space, or scrolled through his Facebook feed on his phone. And then later that day, he'd been performing an extraction and stabbed himself in the thumb. And then he'd had to sew the wound up himself without any numbing agent so he could return to work.

Later that afternoon, I talked to Michell, another of my father's employees, and who had spent the last years of my mother's life driving up to the house in the mornings to help get her bathed, dressed, and fed. Michell told me that she suspected that the woman I'd bumped into in the grocery store had a tendency to exaggerate. But, nevertheless, Dad *was* worried about the lights. My question was: Why hadn't I known?

"He mentioned something about them being demonic," she said, "but I told him I didn't think they were. I told him it was nature sending comfort to him. Think about the Christmas star," she told him. "Or lightning bugs! I told him to try to watch them with a grateful heart. But I don't know that he can. And maybe it has something to do with the fact that every time he tries to take a picture, every time he so much as touches a finger to his phone, they go out. It's not so much what he says about the lights as the look on his face when he talks to you about them. I don't think I've ever seen him that shook up. It's enough to scare the crap out of you!"

I showed Evan the lay of the land. I grabbed a machete and a walking stick and we hit the trails, most of which were overgrown. The blade tinged as I sliced through branches. We dipped into a rhododendron thicket, climbed a steep trail—one that my father had carried my great grandmother up over three decades before, so she could see the view—and walked through whispering grass along an old logging road at the ridge top. I showed him the lookout rock, the one where you could view blue ridges retreating like frozen waves in the distance, and explained, as my father always had, that if you looked at the furthest one out, you could see into Tennessee. We wound back down another trail that passed under a buzzing electrical tower, reached the driveway, and walked along the creek. I pointed out the pool where I had been baptized: the spot where, on May 25, 1985, I donned a zip-up robe over my clothes and walked into the frigid, waist-high water. My father had wrenched rocks from the creek bed and placed them on shelves of dirt he'd dug to create stairs leading down to a glade of trees he'd cleared atop a rock ledge where he'd later set up chairs so the audience would have a place to sit. Across the creek, on another, lower shelf of stone, the flames of a campfire had crackled. Church members aimed their cameras. I was the star of this performance, the brave wader into running water, as I imagined Jesus himself had done when John the Baptist invited him into the Jordan to be baptized. The pastor, a mustachioed man from Michigan who liked country music and referred to ice cream cones as "cones a cream," and with whom I had spent the last few months completing preparatory lessons in a so-called *Baptismal Study Guide*, helped me to his side. I gazed back at the audience as they finished the final lines of "Shall We Gather at the River?" I felt the pastor's hand on my shoulder. He said the magic words. He placed a hand-kerchief over my face and lowered me into the water, and brought me back up. In a rush, it was over. I climbed out of the creek and stood by the blazing fire as my father helped remove my robe and wrapped towels around me. On the other side of the creek, my mother snapped pictures. I would have loved to have said a warmth spread through my body, or that a beam of sunlight fell through the canopy above and bathed me in radiance. I would have liked to report that I felt lighter, forgiven, transformed. What I felt: the heat of the fire, the sting of the frigid creekwater sliding from my head down my spine. The triumphant notes of whatever song the congregation was singing entered and exited my head. I'd been baptized. I could now take a cracker and a thimbleful of grape juice during Communion Sabbath, and I could close my eyes and chew the cracker thoughtfully, as I had seen my parents and other church members do, and I could use a silver basin to wash another man's feet during the ordi-nance of humility. I would glimpse the white, blue-veined, barnacled feet of the other men, watch them slip off their dark JCPenny socks, whose elastic had left streaky imprints on their legs and I would stand afterwards with the men of our congregation and utter publicly a sentence or two of gratitude for what the Lord had done in my life. I would feel overwhelmed, sometimes to the point of terror, that I had nothing to say, or that someone would say what I had been planning to share, or that whatever I had to say would sound phony or insincere. But I wouldn't feel changed. And I feared that, because of that, I would never improve.

For a long time after the sun went down, Evan and I saw only darkness. And stars. For a while, we were fine with that. There were so many—twice, three times more than what you could see at night in Blacksburg, a town that, despite its small size, churned out its fair share of light pollution. I nixed the aluminum foil packet idea and fried up the potatoes, onions, and peppers in one of my mom's frying pans in the kitchen: a yellow corning ware skillet I remembered mom using whenever she scrambled eggs. We roasted hot dogs on metal prongs my father kept for just such an occasion. We chowed down on our s'mores. We poured ourselves glasses of whiskey and gazed into the dark woods. Other than the stars, the only light I could see was coming from the flames licking the inside belly of the chiminea on the front porch.

"Anything?" Lil Evan asked.

"Nothing," I replied.

My father sent me a text from Chicago. He wanted to know what we could see.

Nothing, I replied.

You're kidding, he texted. *Hold on. I'm going to call the house phone.*

He called.

I answered.

"You haven't seen anything at all?" he said.

"Nope."

"Go to the window by my bed and look out from there."

I motioned for Evan to follow me. We crossed through the living room and into the sunporch. The room where my parents had taken to sleeping, so they could drift to sleep listening to the roar of the creek. The room where my mother had died and where, that night, my father had dutifully slept by her side.

Where are you going to sleep tonight? I'd asked him.

I guess I'm gonna sleep where I've slept for the last fifty-two years, he'd said. And he had. I'd thought it was weird at first. Creepy, even. And then: beautiful.

Now, I covered my brow with my hands and peered, through the glass, out the window.

Nothing.

"I don't see anything," I said.

"Open the window," my father directed.

I opened it. Looked out.

The very moment I raised the window, there appeared in the distance a single bright light. It blinked. And then it blinked again. And again. On and off, every few seconds.

"Holy shit. Oh my God, Evan," I said. "Come look at this shit."

Evan joined me at the open window. "Damn," he said.

I moved my head a few inches higher and looked out the window glass, in the exact same direction. Nothing. I looked through an adjacent window which also had not been raised, again in the same direction. Nothing. We returned to the front porch. Nothing. We returned to the sunporch, closed the window. Nothing. We raised the window. A single bright light. It blinked. We tried various positions and angles, but only when our heads were level with the open window—the level at which my dad, waking in the middle of the night, would've raised his own high enough to peer outside the window, which he always kept open while he slept, no matter how cold outside—did the light appear. Lil Evan and I watched it for hours, counting how many times it blinked, then losing count.

That night, I slept in my parents' bed. I slept, like my father, on the right-hand side. Periodically, I'd wake and look out. The light would always be there, in the same place, blinking intermittently. A single bright dot of light that would sometimes dim slightly, as if shielded or filtered by something, but only momentarily, only for a few rounds of blinks. The light appeared nowhere else but that one place. Off to the left, in the distance, along a ridgeline. No ghost leaves. No big light. Just a bright light that blinked. On multiple occasions, I attempted to capture on video what we were watching. The light didn't seem to mind; it continued to blink brightly as I filmed. But each time I replayed the video, even though I could hear Evan as he counted "one...two...three," to keep track of each time we spotted a flash, nothing appeared on the screen but darkness. The half-life of the light could live only in my memory. The only evidence, then, would be Evan's and my eyewitness account. Which, I supposed, was okay. I didn't need to verify its existence to anyone but myself.

My entire life, ever since I'd been a child, I'd been hearing about miracles: the parting of the Red Sea, the falling walls of Jericho, Jonah's survival in the great whale, Jesus walking on water, turning water into wine, Moses standing before the burning bush and hearing the Lord say, "I AM." As a kid, I'd prayed for miracles. So desperate was I to see and experience something that I couldn't explain, I even once prayed—as a kid—to the devil. "Dear Satan," I'd whispered, while hunting lizards in my backyard. "Please help me catch this one." But other than the time I'd been driving in the rain with my friend Tom and we'd hydroplaned and began to spin and it looked like we were headed into oncoming traffic, and I'd imagined the semi-truck headed our way turning us to jelly, until we somehow ended up in the middle lane, I hadn't witnessed any phenomenon to which I might lend the adjective *supernatural*. But I sure did want to. And according to Professor Gritsner, if I kept my eyes open, I just might.

V. DEVIL IN THE DETAILS

A few days after Lil Evan and I had witnessed the blinking light, U.S. passengers from the *Diamond Princess* cruise ship, where an outbreak of the coronavirus had resulted in a quarantine, were evacuated and flown from Tokyo to their homes in the states. Team LeBron beat Team Giannis. More than 1,100 Department of Justice officials called for Attorney General William Barr to step down. And my father, having returned home from Chicago, texted to let me know that the "Big Light" had returned.

According to my father, the light had been moving slowly, roving around the cove, in the big field that sits on the other side of the creek.

Did you use the binoculars? I texted back.

My father said no. I asked why not. He said he could see the light just fine without them.

That's strange, I texted back. *Most curious man I know unexplained phenomena = shrug?*

Who says it's unexplained.

You have an explanation? I replied. *Please share.*

My phone rang. The screen said *Dad*. I answered.

"Yo," I said.

"Hey."

"So, what's the deal?"

"You told me several years ago," he said, "that you didn't believe in the devil."

I neither confirmed nor denied this; I couldn't remember ever having had this particular conversation with my father, though I'd conducted enough of research to understand that the image of Satan as a horned, winged, goatee-wearing imp with a tail and carrying a pitchfork represented a human fiction and that the story my church had told me about the origin of the devil—that he'd been the leader of the heavenly choir, fourth in command, after the Father, Son, and Holy Ghost, and subsequently a general of a great rebellion and loser of a war in heaven that had sent one third of the angels to live on earth—was, in fact, extra-biblical.

I didn't bother telling my father any of this. And I wouldn't remember with much clarity the particulars of his argument, but it went something like this: those lights had supernatural qualities. They seemed to be watching him as much as he'd been watching them. And they understood things, for instance, that whenever he reached for his phone that he intended to photograph them. And they didn't want, for whatever reasons, to be photographed. Moreover, their mere presence was a kind of distraction. And possibly a kind of dangerous seduction or enchantment. There was nothing specific in the bible about such a phenomenon. But it was confusing. A possible deception. And if one could be sure of one thing, it was that God never deceived. Therefore, it seemed likely that the lights were demonic in origin.

I tried to explain to my father that there were a lot of things the Bible failed to explain. And that for all of recorded history, humans had been attributing demonic powers to phenomena they couldn't understand—at their peril. Ailments and illnesses that humans now cured with medicine were once thought to have been brought about by evil spirits. Giordano Bruno, the sixteenth century Italian philosopher, had been burned at the stake for refusing not to believe that the universe was finite and that other solar systems existed. People used to say "bless you" after a person sneezed to prevent the devil from entering their mouths. My own father would never have avoided walking under a ladder. He wouldn't have turned the other way if a black cat crossed his path, or tossed salt over his shoulder were he to spill the shaker. So why was he saying all this shit about the devil?

The word "light"—including variances such as "lightning" or "lighten"—occurs 263 times in the New Revised Standard Version of the Hebrew bible and New Testament. In fact, light was the first particular thing God was said to create, when he formed the heavens and the earth: "And God said, 'Let there be light, and there was light.'" From the very beginning, then, according to God himself, light was good. When the Israelites fled from Egypt, it was God who appeared as a cloud during the day and a pillar of fire at night to light their way. The psalmist praises God for turning his darkness into light. For him, the Lord is his light and salvation—therefore who should he fear? In Psalm 29:7, the Lord strikes with flashes of lightning. In Psalm 119:105, the word of the Lord is a lamp for the Psalmist's feet, a light for his path. In Proverbs 15:30, light is said to bring joy to the heart and in Ecclesiastes 2:13, light is "better" than darkness. The writer of Matthew depicts Jesus as telling his audience to "let their lights shine before others," that they may see the good deeds and glorify their father in heaven. In the Gospel of Luke, Jesus says that a person's eye is the "lamp" of one's body. When eyes are healthy, the whole body is full of light. But when they are unhealthy, the body is also full of darkness. The gospel of John begins by saying that, "In the beginning was the Word, and the Word was with God. He was with God in the beginning. Through him all things were made; without him nothing was made that has been made. In him was life, and that life was the light of all mankind. The light shines in the darkness and the darkness has not overcome it." Light is, according to the bible, good. It is a metaphor for truth. For knowing. Light exposes. Light refines. It's a bright light that blinds Saul on his way to persecute Christians. God calls his people out of darkness and into the "wonderful light." When Peter is visited by an angel in jail, a light shines in his cell, and chains fall from his wrists. In nearly every instance, writers of scripture describe light as not only a positive thing, but often as the best possible thing. Only once is light depicted as dangerous, in Paul's second letter to the Corinthians; here, he warns the church against false prophets and those who masquerade as apostles of Christ: "And no wonder," Paul writes, "for Satan himself masquerades as an angel of light."

The NRSV version of the Holy Bible has more than 700 thousand words. The word "Lord" appears 7,443 times. "God" 475. "Jesus" 1,091. "Angel" 290. "Holy Spirit" 111. The word "Satan" appears 47 times, 14 of those are in the Book of Job. The word "devil" appears on 36 occasions. Compare those numbers to Moses (837), David (1023), Noah (57), Joshua (210), Elijah (108), Isaiah (67) or Abraham (266). Whatever you want to say or claim about Satan, the truth is pretty clear: in holy scripture, he plays but a minor role.

"It doesn't mean he doesn't exist," my sister said, over the phone. She didn't seem to care about the number of times that the word "Satan" or "devil" appeared in the bible. Neither did my brother-in-law, who assured me that it all added up to something and that the reason Ellen G. White the nineteenth-century prophetess and co-founder of the Seventh-day Adventist church—was so focused on Satan was because he was Christ's enemy and the fate of the universe was at stake. I tried to tell him that the dragon in Revelation might not actually refer to Satan and he said, "So what is it? An actual dragon?"

My brother-in-law told me that God used humans to write the Bible and that the reason he hadn't simply spelled out Satan's role in the Bible had everything to do with the fact that the book's true meaning could only be determined through prayer and with the guidance of the holy spirit.

"What do you think about prayer?" my brother-in-law said. "Do you pray?"

I told him I did. But my prayers were not the kind that asked for things—I refused to treat God like Santa Claus. I preferred Simone Weil's definition: "attention, taken to its highest degree, is the same thing as prayer. It presupposes faith and love. Absolutely unmixed attention is prayer. If we turn our mind toward the good, it is impossible that little by little the whole soul will not be attracted thereto in spite of itself."

I'd been pacing up and down my driveway, talking animatedly and saying, "Jesse, that's not in the Bible! It's just not!" This had prompted my wife, who no doubt could hear me through our bedroom window, to text me, *Are you arguing with your sister about religion? That's going to go nowhere. You should stop.*

I texted her back: *It's not my sister. It's Jesse.*

And she texted, *What's the point? Find a way to end on a nice note and stop. We love them. We cannot change their minds about anything.*

As usual, Kelly was right.

My intention in talking about the lights in reference to dad was only meant to downplay their supposed evil, I texted my sister. *Maybe they are evil. Who knows. I just don't think so. And I want dad not to worry. That's all. We've always thought of that property as kind of sacred and beautiful and he certainly has done nothing to summon so-called 'demonic powers.' So I don't think he deserves to entertain those thoughts. Idk. What do I know. Anyway, I love you and don't care if your beliefs are different than mine. Like I told Jesse: maybe this comes from insecurity on my part of being different and thinking differently than how I was raised. I have problems and I project them onto others. I'm sorry and I don't want to disrespect you because I love you. But I'll probably say some things that are antagonistic in the future. Just remind me that I love you and I'll shut up.*

Hahaha, my sister replied. *I love you Matthew and I'm just glad we can talk and we might get heated sometimes but that's ok I know you love me (thinking emoji face) jk I do—and you know how I feel about you. We are all trying to figure things out. That is for sure.*

She ended her message with a heart emoji, and our conversation was over.

"I remember reading somewhere," Big Evan—the professor—
said, "that the chance that light would exist in our universe
is infinitesimally small."

We were sitting in the living room of the tiny saltbox house
where Big Evan lived on Montgomery Street in Blacksburg. I
was talking about the lights and about my family's assertion
that they might be demonic. And now Big Evan was offering
me his thoughts as he sucked periodically, as he always did,
upon the vape pen that resembled a miniature lightsaber
handle and hung from a string around his neck. "I mean,
it's confounding that light even exists, right? Light travels as
both particle and wave? Right? That's confounding. Nothing
else does that. You know, it's weird the way science catches
up to religion and spirituality and the bible. The mystery of
light is something that's been thought about forever."

"That's why I just said, 'according to holy scripture, light
is the best thing there is.'"

"Yeah," Big Evan replied. "It's the best thing and impossible to understand. The best thing is the most mysterious
thing. You take two particles, photons say, light, and they're
spinning positively, one is spinning to the right positively
and the other is spinning to the left negatively and their rota-
tion is dependent upon one another, and if this one gets
looked at, or something happens and its spin changes, then
the other one changes, right? They're entangled, right? You
take those two particles and you begin to move them apart.
And you move them farther apart and farther apart, and
now they've done experiments, one is on this side of the
planet the other one's on this side of the planet. Right? And
you look at that one or you do something to change its spin

and that other one that's on the other side of the planet immediately its spin changes and it happens instantaneously. It happens faster than the speed of light. You could put one of those particles on one side of the universe and another at the other side of the universe and you change one and the other immediately goes, but the speed of light is supposed to be a speed limit, and it doesn't pertain there. And that's why Einstein said that shit's impossible. But it's been demonstrated throughout experiments to be true."

Light, I thought again. *The best thing there is.* This felt true to me, as it did every time I acknowledged it. I thought about starlight. Firelight. Bulbs on Christmas trees. City skylines after dark. The little node at the end of an anglerfish's modified dorsal spine that acted as a fishing lure. The moon, on a cloudless night. Was there anything *better*, more necessary than *light*? Love, maybe, but you couldn't have love without light. And you needed just the right amount. You needed a star. One with a radius of about 423,690 miles. And then, about 92 million miles from that sun, you needed a giant conglomeration of oxygen, silicon, aluminum, iron, calcium, sodium, potassium, and magnesium. You needed a crust. A mantle. An outer and inner core. You needed water and wind and plants and insects and reptiles and fish and mammals. Bleeding tooth fungus! Venus flytraps! Jellyfish! Platypuses! Elephants! None of which would ever have existed had it not been for this one essential thing we couldn't seem to really understand or explain, as if at the heart of existence, whatever made us had placed a giant question mark, so that we, as the only species on a rock orbiting a far-away but just-close-enough source of light who were capable of engaging in the art of sustained reflection, would never run out of questions.

VI. THE MEANING OF LIGHT

My father awoke in the middle of the night. The big light was back, illuminating the hickory tree. But this time, no green leaves appeared anywhere. Instead, he said, the top of the tree was covered with what looked like bubbles.

"I woke up to that twice," he said. "It was like a bubble bath type thing."

"Did you pinch yourself?" I asked.

"I didn't have to," he said. "It was interesting. I got up to go to the bathroom and it went away. There was definitely a light on it, but the bubbles obstructed it. You could see the limbs in places. The bubbles were white. Once I got up and the light went off, the tree was bare. Sky was full of these fluffy clouds and it looked like what had been on the tree. The shapes of the clumps of bubbles and stuff. Up in the sky instead of the tree. It's almost always dark when I go to bed but as soon as I'm there for about three to five minutes, a light starts blinking. In the same place. Until I touch my phone. And then it stops."

I couldn't shut up about the lights. I went out of my way to tell everyone who'd listen. I made people—my wife, son, friends, colleagues, students—put coats over their heads to block out daylight so they could watch the lights blinking in that initial video that my father had taken. I told them about the big roving beam of light. How the hickory tree had lit up and how, at its very top, green leaves had appeared. How they'd disappeared as soon as my dad reached for his phone. And how I'd stared into the dark with Lil Evan for hours before we opened the window and the single bright light began to flash. I couldn't shut up because I couldn't stop thinking about them. But also? I wanted to hear what other people thought. The lights were enigmatic. Inexplicable. Telling others about them presented me with an occasion to gather perspectives. And for the people I told to reveal what they believed.

A former student, Chera Longfritz, an English and fashion merchandising and design major, stopped by my office to say hello, and so I subjected her, as I did everyone, to the story about the lights.

"Oh my god," Chera said, mouth agape, hand on her heart. "I just got a full-on spine shiver. You know what that is right?"

"Tell me."

"Dude," she said. "That is totally your mom."

I knew Chera would say this. She'd written essays about her own attraction to the unexplained and the paranormal: how, as a child, she'd ask her parents for a flashlight after the sun went down, so that she could embark upon backyard monster hunts. She was the girl at sleepovers who told ghost stories. Perched on her pink *Power Puff Girls* pillow, she'd recite the story of the Moses Grandy Ghost, or "The Woman in my Window," or "The Books that Fell from my Shelf in the Middle of the Night." All these stories she believed then, and now, to be true.

Now, Chera said, she and her dad had a real ghost in their house. All the ghosts she'd once hunted, the ones she'd begged to give her a sign, and that she'd attempted to communicate with on a Hasbro Ouija board her dad bought at Toys"R"Us, couldn't compare to this one. Because this ghost?

This ghost was her mother.

"Angie."

According to Chera, her intensive knowledge of ghosts stemmed from watching horror movies, reading creepypasta on Reddit, and studying clips of recorded audio and flickering EMF sensors on YouTube. If she truly believed that someone could walk into a haunted hotel where someone died in room 113 and communicate with the spirit of the dead, why couldn't her mom's spirit be floating through their house, waiting for the right moment to manipulate the light switch or cut off the TV?

Because that was another thing Chera believed ghosts could do: manipulate electrical energy.

"Think of it like this," she told me. "Ghosts are living in another *realm*, on an entirely different *plane*. Of *course*, they can't just give you a pat on the back and say, 'Hey buddy, how's it going?' Don't be ridiculous! Instead, they store up their ghostly energy to enter our living realm through electromagnetic fields."

Ah, I thought. *Of course.*

So, when Chera's dad called to tell her that he swore up and down that he'd left the lights on before he went to sleep because he'd been too tired to turn them off, but found them all switched off when he woke up the next morning, she believed him.

"That was Mom telling you to turn the damn lights off," she said.

This made Chera and her dad cry-laugh. Once upon a time, her mother had been "so anal" about saving electricity. Now, she was controlling it.

I told Chera how weird it was: that ever since my own mother died, I felt like I sensed her presence almost everywhere I went.

"Same," she said. She felt her mom's presence, like, constantly. Whether it was an electric bulb flickering or a bird flying nearby or a butterfly grazing her finger, she found her mother in the tiny, everyday things of life. Out of nowhere, signs of her mother's presence appeared everywhere. A rustling of leaves behind her at the bus stop. A funky shaped cloud. Just, like, all the time.

Christmas 2019 was Chera's second Christmas without her mom, but somehow it felt like the first; the previous Christmas her mother's death had been so fresh that the incessant talking about her absence made the woman feel present in a weirdly palpable way.

Every year, Chera and her mom decorated the Christmas tree together. It was their thing. Their ritual. They always chose a crazy "anti-Christmas" theme, like pink and purple butterflies or peacocks or birds or sunflowers. Chera's mom could find a way to make anything fashionable, and Chera loved shopping with her to hunt down the most random décor. Though her dad never helped, they could always count on him to show up at the end and say, "Wow, that looks great!"

This year, however, Chera's father had thrown away almost all of the family's Christmas decorations. Without asking permission. And so Chera had come home to empty red and green boxes and a look on her dad's face similar to a dog's when it's taken a giant shit on the living room rug. Immediately, she knew that he'd thrown them away in a moment of panic, maybe because he'd remembered her mom's face too clearly and the smell of her cooking cinnamon rolls on Christmas morning. He apologized. Chera forgave him. Still, it hurt.

For whatever reason, Chera's dad had not thrown out the electric snowmen, the ones that, when plugged in, glowed red to green to blue and back again. Those snowmen had been part of the Christmas decor at the Longfritz house for as long as Chera could remember. They looked old too. Like they'd been plugged into their fair share of outlets. Chera decided to plug them in right next to her mother's urn, which sat atop the cabinet in the family's dining room.

They stayed plugged in for about a week before Christmas. Every morning Chera passed the dining room and noted the twinkling lights, and paused to grant her mother's grey marble vase a kiss. She even placed a pair of green and red fuzzy socks atop the urn; her mother's feet had always been notorious for freezing and cramping.

On Christmas Eve, when Chera and her dad were driving home from her grandma's, they talked about how they couldn't wait to go inside their house and greet their new puppies, maybe watch an episode of *The Office*, drink a few glasses of wine, and wake up the next morning anytime they wanted.

"Who cares about waking up early, let's do whatever we want," Chera's dad said, and thus it was decided: Christmas would officially become their "Who Gives a Fuck?" holiday. It was better than pretending to enact all the traditions they had done with Chera's mom. Instead? They'd make their own.

That night, before they went to bed, they turned off all the lights. They turned the alarm on. They gathered the doggies and started up the stairs.

That's when the ringing began. It came in sets of three high-pitched chimes, then a few seconds of silence, three more chimes. Silence, chimes. Silence, chimes.

Also? It was *loud*.

"Where is that coming from?" Chera asked. She searched the upstairs. Her room. The guest bedroom. Her dad's room. His bathroom. Her father searched downstairs. The back deck. The garage.

Chera returned downstairs and headed toward her mom's ashes. The ringing seemed to be growing louder, and when she reached the urn, it was clear. The sound was coming from the lit-up snowmen. They'd been plugged in for a week but they hadn't once made a sound. In fact, Chera had never heard them make any kind of noise, ever. That night, though, they rang and rang until Chera and her father were standing over her mother's urn. They held each other. They wiped silent tears from their eyes. It had been exactly midnight when they located the source of the ringing. They kissed the urn. They said, "Merry Christmas." Chera unplugged the snowmen and addressed her mother. "I hear you," she said. "I'm sorry I didn't say goodnight before I went upstairs. I miss you, too. I wish you were here. Obviously."

Chera told me that she hoped her mother's spirit would continue to haunt her. And she didn't use the word *haunt* negatively. In fact, when she was little, she secretly hoped that one of the monsters or ghosts she encountered would attach itself to her body. Then she could spook her friends. Maybe, one day down the line, she could form an intimate relationship with the ghost.

Chera guessed that her wish had come true, albeit in a really fucked up way. Now, though, she felt like she could call upon the power of her mom whenever she needed it most, asking her advice through whispers under her breath, or seeing her mother's name on a car license plate when she was feeling extra lonely.

According to Chera, her mom's spirit lived in the pocket of her jeans. She lived in the Blue Ridge Mountains. She lived on Main Street in Blacksburg. She lived in her dad's closet at home, rearranging his shoes at night. She lived in the electrical wires of her aunt's apartment. She lived in the gas burner of her grandma's stove. Maybe, Chera thought, her mother died so she could be with everyone she loved at once.

I told Chera that the lights at my dad's house seemed to grow stronger every day. Again, Chera said she knew that was my mother. That she'd been storing her energy, using a little each day, growing stronger until she could slam her power into her husband's face, casting light on the tree to yell, "I miss you!"

This, Chera assured me, was absolutely factual.

I told my friend Scott, the rector of the local Blacksburg Episcopal church. Scott was a friend and confidant. He'd presided over the confirmation classes I'd taken after deciding to become a member of the church, and who introduced the theological concept of the "three-legged stool," or the threefold sources of authority in Anglicanism: scripture, tradition, and ritual.

Anglicans believed that if any one of them were to be emphasized more than the other—if one of the "legs" ended up longer than another—then the stool would become unbalanced, unable to stand upright. It was this kind of common-sense approach to religion that attracted me to Anglicanism: that and the fact that the entirety of the church service, aside from a brief homily, was scripted. Going to an Episcopal church, then, felt very literary. Scripture was read, songs were sung from the hymnal, every prayer recited from prayer book. Adventists, I suppose, might be wary of rote recitation—I remember hearing that the prayer "God is great, God is good, let us thank him for our food" wasn't an especially good blessing, because it was something that people recited mindlessly, rather than searching one's heart and letting that shape whatever utterance you improvised. But there's something about coming to the part of the service when everyone, in unison, confesses their sins, and in so doing says, "we have not loved others as ourselves." I liked to imagine that these prayers—measured and precise—were waiting quietly each week to come alive in the mouths of human beings who, no matter how good or kind they might have been, benefitted from the acknowledgement of their own failures and shortcomings.

And how good were they really? How kind? It was easy for me to forget that these same people ate flavorless wafers and drank red wine that they believed represented the blood sacrifice of a god humans killed two thousand years ago and now lived in heaven with a father and spirit god. But these people: they were also good and kind. They sent backpacks filled with toys and candy and pencils and coloring books and toothpaste and toothbrushes and hats and mittens to Lakota children every Christmas. They practiced for Easter pageants that featured one of the foremost Darwin scholars and his wife playing Adam and Eve. They sent high school kids on pilgrimages. They believed in equality for all human beings, no matter the race, gender, creed, or sexual orientation. And they sang solemn, centuries-old hymns that, whenever I joined in, allowed me to feel, at least for a moment, a transcendent joy.

Scott's office, at the back of a narrow hall that faced the church parking lot, was so cozy: walls had been decorated with antique train cars, and books lined shelves, along with other random objects: a miniature replica of Christ Church, and an unopened package of "Believe in God" breath spray, with the tagline: *Surrender yourself to a higher power and never feel alone again!*

Scott was a big man with a salt and pepper beard. On the day I visited, he wore a black eyepatch, thanks to a recent surgery for a detached retina, and this gave him a kind of uncharacteristically roguish appearance.

"So," I said, "you remember that my mother passed away recently."

"Yes," he replied. "I remember that wonderful eulogy that you posted to Facebook."

"Yeah, well, you know, it's weird. Mom was sick for a decade. And we knew how this particular sickness would end. And sometimes, I just wished it would. I didn't like to see her suffer. But then, when she did die, that's when it hit me. This woman whose body in which I had formed and who had birthed me and loved me unconditionally from the moment she met me was gone. And yet at the same time she was everywhere. I thought about her constantly. It was like she had disappeared from the earth and entered it at the same time. And you know me enough to know how I've struggled with evolving beyond the religion I grew up in. Everyone in my family is an Adventist. My aunt—my dad's sister—is married to the president of the church! I've spent a lot of time resenting the fact that my parents sent me to church schools and took me every week to a place where people gathered to sing and pray and which instilled within me the ability to access shame and guilt at any time. But after my mom passed away, all that, like, just disappeared."

"Wow," Scott said.

"Yeah," I replied. "Like the day after mom's memorial service, I remember I was hanging out at my dad's house. Kelly and Elijah had gone back to Virginia. My dad's brother and sister and both their spouses were there. We were eating supper and I was sitting across from my aunt's husband, the aforementioned church president, a man who I've known all my life and has been nothing but nice to me, but whose piety and single-minded devotion to his church has always kind of repulsed me. Suddenly, I just saw him as my uncle. As a person who loved my mom. And who my mom had loved right back. So what if we didn't have the same beliefs? I should love and respect him just the same."

"Sounds like you had a kind of transformational moment."

"Absolutely. So, this has been more or less the world I've been living in ever since she died. I don't know why but I feel full of compassion and a closeness to certain family members that I haven't felt in a long time."

"That's great!"

"Yeah. It is. But that's only the beginning."

I told Scott about the lights. The blinking. The flashing. The floating beam and the hickory tree. I told him how I'd made the trip down to my father's house and for the longest time hadn't seen anything until I followed Dad's instructions. And opened the window.

"So," Scott said, "when you first started talking about the lights appearing to your dad, the first thing that came to my mind was some sense of communication from the world beyond that's separated from this existence by that 'thin veil.' And I'll give you an example: after I had this detached retina surgery, my mother's oldest sister died back in November, and for the last few years of her life was legally blind. And I didn't get to go to her funeral. And in this dream I'd had—Margaret, that was her name—she came to me. She was 93 when she died, but she looked about 40 in the dream, and she never said a word to me. I said to her, 'Oh Aunt Margaret, I'm sorry I never came to your service.' And she hugged me. And that was it. But it was *not* like a dream even though I was asleep. What's happening with your dad is different because he's awake. He's having this experience of this phenomenon. And then, when you were searching for the lights and he said, 'Well, did you open the window?' and somehow that triggers the phenomenon to happen made me think—I always think metaphorically—'Is your window open?' Are you open to having this experience that's about to unfold in front of you—and what does it mean? You know, I still, I wouldn't assign any of that to evil. I think it's probably somehow the work of the divine. Because of the light. And maybe what's being said is, 'How much do I have to do to get you to believe?' That's how I look at it. That it's a positive affirmation of the goodness of what's to come. Are you open to this experience? Because there's nothing going to separate you from the light once that window's open."

"Huh," I said. I hadn't thought of it that way. But I wanted to. I wanted to open myself to the lights. Whatever they were. "So," I continued, "As a person who has much experience in pastoral care, although you probably don't get the chance to give Seventh-day Adventists advice, but knowing a little bit about my dad's theology, what would your advice be that honors what he believes but you know also comforts him?"

"I think I would maybe just make the suggestion—I don't know how Adventists believe in terms of sort of a purposeful God—do things happen for a reason or is it just a free for all?"

"I can't think of a denomination that believes more strongly that everything happens for a reason."

"Then I guess I would say maybe this has happened for a reason and the timing for him to think about the possibilities beyond what he's thought about? I don't want to give it any kind of specific framing, especially if you could point to the whole thing with the hickory tree being illumined with leaves in winter and relate it to the burning bush thing. It's a theophany. And not attribute it to Satan or any kind of evil. But to the divine. That works in light. What it means, I'm not sure. Maybe it is to get him to not be so certain. That there are things in this world and the next that we don't understand. And it's okay. You don't have to have it all pinned down. And perhaps it means that even in the midst of death, we might have the opportunity to find new life."

New life, I thought. Yes. That was it. My mother had

died. And yet she was more alive than ever. And light—light was divine.

On October 20, 1979, near the forty-five-minute mark of *Saturday Night Live*, the actor Eric Idle introduced cast member Andy Kaufman. Kaufman then appeared in a robe and addressed the audience, explaining how he'd been going from town to town, challenging women to wrestling matches, offering $500 to any woman who could beat him. He said that he'd chosen women to wrestle because he was not an athlete, and because he did not believe that a woman could beat a man, a sentiment that elicited groans from the crowd.

"Mopping the floors, raising the babies. I think also the men—[*crowd objects*] The men have let the women come to a higher, you know, a higher position than they're able—I think the men are a bunch of pussy cats and pansies for letting this happen. And I think the men in this country are nothing but pitiful specimens of manhood."

The audience booed.

A bearded Bob Zmuda, wearing a referee's outfit and carrying a microphone, appeared in the frame, asking for female volunteers who might be interested in wrestling Kaufman.

"This is real," he said, "this is not a set up!"

He waved a stack of bills to prove it. Five women lined up onstage.

He asked to wrestle "the tall one." Zmuda pointed to a young woman in the front row, a woman named Mimi Lambert. She wrestled Kaufman valiantly for over three minutes, surviving Kaufman's hair pulling and body slams, jumping onto Kaufman from behind, grabbing his knees and pulling him back onto the mat, and almost pinning him on at least one occasion before Kaufman eventually eked out his victory.

Mimi had come to Western North Carolina to help search for the wife of the owner of a boutique in West Palm Beach who'd gone missing during a vacation in the mountains.

Since 2019, Mimi had been living in the house that my grandparents built in 1982, a quarter of a mile from the house my parents later built and lived ever since. I'd heard about Mimi for months before I met her. "Quite a character," my father said. "Talking to her is about like trying to drink water from a fire hose."

After wrestling Kaufman, Mimi—the stepdaughter of the CEO of Izod Lacoste—had briefly dated him; the two would remain friends until his untimely death. She'd hung out with the *SNL* staff and claimed to have helped with writing a commercial parody for one of the show's episodes. Years later, she'd contracted HIV after a sexual encounter with the heir to a popular beer fortune. She'd been pregnant with twins she'd lost five months into her pregnancy. Once, following Hurricane Gene, she'd attempted to rescue a dog and was subsequently electrocuted by a downed power line. As a fifty-nine-year-old single woman, Mimi had subsequently stumbled into the local Seventh-day Adventist church, befriended my parents, and decided, preferring southwestern North Carolina to South Florida, to rent my grandparents' house, which she filled with artwork and jewels and cookbooks and stacks of high-end fashion wear and sculptures—including one in the shape of a Dachshund that'd been completely composed of random pieces of junk, including a disembodied doll's hand, a fork, a hinge, and a '70s-era Fisher Price Little Person.

I wanted to talk to Mimi because she was one of the only people—besides my dad, Lil Evan, and me—to see the lights. The night she first watched them, she was certain somebody with a flashlight had been standing on the deck outside her bedroom. Hunters, maybe. And then she started seeing flashes of light outside the bedroom where she slept. And on more than one occasion, she awoke to see the woods outside the bay window in her bedroom awash in light, and assumed the sun was rising, but when she walked out of the bedroom and into the living room, she found it dark as night. Back in the bedroom, outside that bay window, it was sunny. In the middle of the night.

Mimi didn't know what it was. But she had a theory.

Before I got judgey or called her crazy, I needed to know that she'd had previous confirmed and documented experience with extraterrestrial life forms.

Of course she had.

Back when Mimi was responsible for helping with the redesign of an apartment that belonged to Bob De Niro, on Hudson Street in Tribeca, she'd spent a weekend roller blading on Nantucket with Robert Arnot, a physician, and Jan Stanbury, an architect. Upon their return from the island, in a private plane on its way back to Manhattan, Arnot began playing his clarinet. As the song unfurled, a silver object— like a helicopter, but different, Mimi said—had appeared in the air outside the window. The passengers, who watched it hover before it sped away, were each detained upon landing, and led into separate rooms by officials who questioned them, recording their accounts, and telling them never to speak again of what they had seen.

Did I know that Hitler—who'd been obsessed with finding lost relics, like the Ark and the Holy Grail—had once commissioned an exploration of Antarctica because he believed that there was a hole there, three miles deep, that might lead to the lost city of Atlantis? And that a pilot, flying above this aperture in the earth, had seen "ships" going in and out of it?

No, I hadn't heard that.

"Look it up," Mimi said. "That's your homework."

I looked it up that night. She was right. The Nazis had gone to Antarctica. Legend had it that they built a city-sized base to host the SS, cults, and occultists, and it was there that they were taught by extraterrestrials to build flying saucers. The facts, however, suggested that while they had made the journey to the south pole, they'd only stayed for about ten days. According to an article titled, "Hitler on Ice: Did the Nazis Have a Secret Antarctic Fortress?" by Matt Soniak, writing for *Mental Floss*, other polar expeditions of the era were known to have taken "twice that long" to build even "small huts."

"You know," Mimi said, "Your father asked me a while ago if I had anything demonic in the house. I told him I didn't, that I'd burned my Kabbalah books, though I did have some Native American baskets and a pipe."

Mimi's great uncle, Manuel Gamio, was a renowned Mexican anthropologist. Often considered as the father of modern anthropological studies in Mexico, he had devised a well-known system for classifying the hunter-gatherers of Central America.

"But I don't consider Native American artifacts to be demonic," Mimi said. "I know some people do."

"You know, Mimi," I said. "Both you and dad sleep in rooms where people have died—my mom in his and my grandfather in yours." I didn't tell her that once my grandmother—the one who wanted me to smother her with a pillow if she ever lost her mind—once saw my dead grandfather walk past the front window, carrying a chainsaw.

"That doesn't scare me," Mimi said.

"So wait," I said. "Remind me. What does that whole Hitler looking for Atlantis have to do with the lights?"

"I don't know," Mimi said. "I just think that the lights might be alien presences. Or beings who might have come from that hole. Maybe they're searching these mountains for rock or stone. You know these are some of the oldest mountains in the world. They're full of all kinds of rocks and minerals. Things that the people who live underground might need."

Again, she said she didn't know. But she wouldn't be surprised if all this stuff was somehow connected.

I wasn't sure about the aliens. Or beings living underground or passageways to other worlds. But the idea of "connected-ness"—that somehow everything was connected, that the universe represented one giant quantum field, or that Earth was an ecosystem upon which the existence of every insect, human, plant, and animal depended—that I took some comfort in. The universe was huge. Even if we traveled the globe constantly, we'd see very little of what was out there. There was so much to understand. But even more that we never would.

Any development with the lights? Jack and Elia wanted to know. Jack and Elia were former students, and I'd told them about the lights when they and several others had stopped by my office the previous week; now, we were standing on the corner of Draper and College Avenues in downtown Blacksburg. It was February 25, 2020. Harvey Weinstein had been found guilty of sex crimes. As the coronavirus spread, U. S. stocks plunged. Bernie Sanders promised to attract new voters. And Jack and Elia leaped out of Bollo's—a local coffee shop, which is tiny and usually crowded—to say hello when they spotted me walking down the street. I'd met Jack and Elia the semester before, in my creative nonfiction workshop. Jack, who had curly hair and big glasses and would be the first to admit that he talked too much, partly because he had a lot to say, and partly because he was so desperately skeptical of all the things he said that he felt compelled to constantly revise and comment on everything he said, even as he was saying it, had written a funny essay that dramatized his dancing skills— or lack thereof. Elia, who had a pierced nose and wore gold rimmed glasses, flowy clothes, and purple Doc Martens, and worked at the Moss Arts Center, guarding sculptures made out of repurposed truck tires, had once written, during an in-class exercise, about a boy who'd told her he'd thought it was "so hot" that she hardly ever looked at her phone. My favorite thing that Elia had written, however, was an essay about going to see the hardcore metal band Slayer.

I summarized for Jack and Elia my recent discussion, via phone, with my father, sister, and brother-in-law. How we'd argued about the extent to which the lights seemed demonic. How I'd tried to explain that the word "light," at least in scripture, had always been a good thing. How little the bible talked about or made reference to Satan. How, despite the fact that we'd disagreed vociferously with each other, we'd ended the conversations peaceably.

Jack pushed out his bottom lip and nodded. "So," he said. "Wow. Dialogue. That seems healthy."

Elia, her brow furrowed with concern, nodded. She was wearing a crocheted pair of white, fingerless gloves, a detail that made me remember how she'd once said that she thought of herself as a chameleon; sometimes she liked to dress like a hippie. Sometimes a punk rocker. Sometimes a conservative Mennonite from Central Virginia.

"All in all," Jack added, "it was probably a good thing. Right?"

"Probably," I said, shrugging.

"You know what I think?" Jack said. He unleashed a conspiratorial smile.

"What?"

Jack wagged a finger. "I think the lights are a *test*."

"Oh yeah?" I replied.

"Absolutely. For both you and your dad."

"You know," I said, "You really should consider a career in the ministry."

"Ha," Jack said, grinning. "That's what my mom always tells me."

"What do you mean though?"

"I don't know." Jack rested a hand thoughtfully upon his chin. "I just think that's what it is. A test. You've got a man who has an answer for everything and another man," he paused to nod at me, "who's struggling to find his place in his family."

Behind us, two Jehovah's Witnesses stood nearly motionless beside a rack of magazines. A sign at the top of the stand said, ARE YOU SEARCHING FOR TRUTH?

Elia, after glancing at the evangelists, said she wondered what they—the Witnesses—were feeling. This seemed to me a very Elia thing to say. Maybe because I'd heard her ask something similar when I'd told her and the other students about the lights. "What does your dad think?" she'd asked.

"What do you mean?" I'd replied.

"Like, how does he *feel* about seeing the lights?" It'd been a good question. One that hadn't, for whatever reason, occurred to me to ask.

"Maybe you should ask them how *they're* feeling," I suggested, nodding toward the Witnesses.

"Maybe," Elia said. But she didn't want to talk to them. Not now. She had stories for her fiction class to read. And Jack had a presentation on Celtic linguistics to finish. I bade them adieu, promised I'd keep them posted, and headed to my office, the word "test" flashing in my head, over and over. I'd never liked tests. Never been all that good at taking them in school. I didn't much like tests of faith, either. Abraham agreeing to sacrifice his own son because the Lord had told him to. Satan wagering that Job would curse God's name if God took everything he loved away from him. I didn't know if Jack was right, but also? He didn't seem wrong. It was at least one way of thinking about the lights. What did you make of something you couldn't explain? Any explanation was a kind of test, a trial. The word "test," as a noun, was from the late fourteenth century. Back then, a test was a "small vessel used in assaying precious metals," from old French, derived from Latin meaning "earthen pot." It kind of made sense. Strange lights had appeared—were appearing—in my dad's woods and everybody who knew about them was attempting to ascertain what they were. Or maybe they—the lights—were attempting to make sense of us.

VII. LIGHT BEAM GENERATOR

Because I had a couple hundred dollars of annual research money to burn, and because I had sought to obtain as many interpretations of the lights as possible, I made an appointment on March 9, 2020, for a Zoom session with Luisa, a shamanic psychotherapist who was quarantining in Spain. I initiated this meeting in my office in the English department at Virginia Tech, where we were not yet quarantining. It was spring break. The building was nearly vacant. Even so, I taped a sign on my door that said, PLEASE DO NOT DISTURB. Luisa was wearing a black blouse with a pattern of what appeared to be red roses. It matched her lipstick. We greeted one another, exchanged pleasantries, acknowledged that we were living in crazy times. I told her that I wanted to get her take on a strange phenomenon that I'd witnessed. She said, "Okay" and asked if I wanted to begin by doing some "work." I took that to mean "shamanic work" and agreed.

Ten years before, I'd driven from Blacksburg, Virginia to Santa Fe, New Mexico, to visit Luisa for the first time. As I'd explained it to the chair of the English department, who'd suggested I use the start-up funds I'd been given as a new assistant professor to embark upon some kind of project, the purpose of my trip was to conduct research. And in a sense, it had been. I'd been working on a novel about a boy who, having lived the first thirteen years of his life without knowing the identity of his father, discovers that the man was a shaman living in New Mexico. But the truth was, I didn't give a shit about the novel. I wanted to embark upon a purposeful journey. I wanted magic and mysticism. Or, at the very least, a collision with the ineffable.

Luisa did not, upon greeting me at her front door, look like a shaman. She wore a dark shirt, open at neck, dangly earrings, jeans, and cowboy boots. She asked me what interested me about shamanic activity and non-ordinary reality. I talked about my writing, and that I'd done some research, read some books, one of which had been Michael Harner's *The Way of the Shaman*. I was simply interested, I said, in having a shamanic experience, but honestly, I'd also been feeling some resistance, probably due to my upbringing, and that even though I was no longer a member of the Seventh-day Adventist church, I could never completely escape its influence.

"Oh my god," Luisa said.

"What?"

"Literally the second you mentioned Adventism, I watched a tentacle unfurl from the ceiling and enter the top of your head."

"Seriously?" I looked at the ceiling. No tentacle.

"Yeah. But it's okay. I've seen similar things when working with Mormon clients. The important thing is that you're open to these energies. That I can sense." Luisa asked me to sit Indian-style on the couch and to focus on the area below my belly button, to bring air in and imagine it entering my body at that location. Then she asked me to breathe through my mouth, breathing deeply and focusing on my stomach and my spine.

"In our culture," she said, "this isn't really how we're focused. We're focused outward and forward and upward. Not down and back. So don't look out. Look *in*."

She guided me through some breathing and imaginative exercises.

"I'm picking up something," she said. "From maybe when you were six years of age. Does that resonate?"

"I don't know, honestly."

"Okay. I'm going to do a diagnostic interpretation. I work a lot with shadow souls. You know about chi?"

"Sort of."

"Well, it's life force. And sometimes the flow can get stuck."

Luisa began banging on a drum and asked me to imagine myself absorbing the energy of the drum.

She stopped abruptly. "Wisdom soul," she said. "You lost it at age six. It didn't take much. You were a curious child. Beyond your years, it seems. At some point, I don't know exactly how, you ventured outward. Beyond what, perhaps, your family or church deemed acceptable. And your father, as gently as possible, corrected you. That's when this part of you—the wisdom soul—left."

Luisa smiled. She said she could see my six-year-old self. He was wearing what looked to be a cowboy suit and had been living, all this time, on a dude ranch in what looked like Montana. He'd liked living there because the sky was so big. Even so, he wanted to come home. But in order to do that, he would need to bring the sky with him.

"Do you want him to come back?" Luisa asked.

"Yes," I said.

She smudged me with sage smoke and a feather. She wanted me to say "welcome" to the six-year-old boy. So I did. She rattled all around me. On the backs of my closed eyelids, flashes of light—or fire—appeared.

"I can see that your family's given you a lot of love," she said. "You've been given a lot of good things by your childhood religion. That isn't always the case."

And then the session was over. I wasn't sure how I felt or what to think. As much as I'd enjoyed my time with Luisa— the sensation of a benevolent stranger guiding me through various breathing and thought exercises had left me feeling grounded and refreshed—I remained somewhat skeptical. I now had a little boy living inside me? On the one hand, it sounded preposterous. But I liked imagining it. I left Luisa's house with my six-year-old wisdom soul intact, and a baggy of tobacco she'd instructed me to sprinkle at the feet of a "grandfather tree." I never did.

Ten years later, I told Louisa the whole story in my office. About my mother's illness. About my father's near superhuman capacity for patience and compassion while taking care of her. About my mother's death and how, suddenly, she was everywhere in the world. About how much I missed her. And how the resentment I'd nursed about certain members of my family—namely the most conservative—seemed to have dissolved in the days following her passing, because I realized I didn't have to care about what anyone else believed, especially when they claimed to love me. I told her about the lights. How Lil Evan and I had gone to see them and we couldn't until we entered my parents' room and opened the window. About Dad observing the green leaves in the hickory tree. About the Big Light and that my father worried that all these unexplained energies might have an evil origin story. Luisa wrote all this down.

Following her instructions, I closed my eyes. I massaged the space beneath my earlobes and along my jawline. I used my fingers to comb energy from the sides of my face and flick it away. I imagined a core like a riverbed that ran through my body: a plumb-line from the crown of my head down to the perineum. I breathed. Luisa asked me to note the location of my most palpable emotional sensations. "So," she said. "The lower solar plexus. Okay, bring both your hands to rest on the solar plexus. I'm going to give you a checklist of emotions and you can tell me what you're feeling in that area." I wasn't feeling love, passion, anger, fear, guilt, or shame. But I was feeling joy.

Luisa asked me to reimagine the window in my parents' bedroom.

"Good, she said. "Now lift up that window. And I want you to imagine you have the window in your dad's room. Unlatch it and then push it up. Good. Does it stay up by itself?"

"Yes."

Luisa began drumming. I closed my eyes. I saw the red frame of a window. Darkness. Splotches. Every once in a while, a flash of light appeared.

After she finished, and without saying a word, Luisa picked up a pen and began writing vigorously on a yellow legal pad. She was beaming, as if she'd seen something beautiful and couldn't help herself.

———————

"Okay," she finally said, "I felt—wow—I had a very...it wasn't painful but I had this powerful and bittersweet wave of emotion move through me. That's when I felt your mother's presence and energy. And the first thing I noticed was this: I really felt as though I was *with* her. There was this palpable sense of liberation and excitement and—oh my God. Like she'd had a profound spiritual experience during the last ten years of her life. Like *profound*. Her last ten years were rich. Maybe not from your and my way of seeing things. But on *this* level? The one I just experienced with her? Far from that. I mean I already think your mom was one of these people who's a kind of light beam generator—oh! Did you hear what I just *fucking* said?"

"Wow."

"And in those last ten years of her life, she experienced love on a profound level. Obviously from your dad. Because you couldn't ask for a more loyal and loving and compassionate and authentic companion than that."

"Exactly."

"What I also wrote in my notes was...she found the light. And she desperately wants your dad to know that life is so much bigger than he imagines. Like, I felt this sense of—excitement isn't quite the word but this *happiness* because of your receiving these unusual visitations, because *you* have given them the loving attention of your own inquiry. It's as if the essence of your mom, what's your mom's first name?"

"Sandra."

"It's as if Sandra is so grateful that you've noticed and that you're looking deeper. But actually? This is more for your dad."

"Huh."

"And if this is as far as your dad gets with this in this lifetime, something quite amazing has happened. He may think it's the devil but I think that in the core of himself, some window has been opened. And like you were saying earlier, his adherence to the church was based on his perception that this was the most logical, rational, sensible way he could possibly kind of organize his life and his beliefs."

"Right."

"And so, something else that loud and clear through this continued presence that I see as connected with your mom: she would like to move on to what she called the 'Big Light.' And so, this—these lights—will not continue indefinitely. Because she's still kind of earthbound, Matthew. And it's intentional. She's keeping part of her electromagnetic field in this astral dimension. But she wants to move on. This is an act of love. This is, and is not a sacrifice. She's just like, *I so want you to get this.* But I would hope for her sake that it does not continue indefinitely, unless she has some kind of know-how that I don't know about where she could, let's say, merge with the 'Big Light,' as she calls it. The inclusion of this development in your manuscript feels…purposeful? I'll read you what I wrote. And I might say this came from Sandra. This light cannot be perceived through a filter. Or through glass. Windows ultimately act as mirrors, whether we perceive our own reflections in them or not. So that closed window in the glass, and I suppose the mirrors are always reflecting my own image back to me."

"Right."

"And then, what I received and heard was, 'including this in your manuscript will open more windows.'"

"It already has."

"Beautiful."

"One last question," I said. "If I find myself in the presence of this again, is there anything beyond doing what I've done in the past that you would recommend?"

"I'd say thank you. And I get it. I receive it, Mom."

I promised that's what I would do.

VIII. REMEMBERED JOYS ARE NEVER PAST

The tip of the middle finger on my left hand has been dead ever since September 12, 2019, the day I helped lower my mother's coffin into her grave.

About forty people stood in the family cemetery. It was hot. My shirt—a collared polo I'd borrowed from my father's closet, because I hadn't thought to bring anything resembling a dress shirt—was flooded with sweat. Gnats pulsed in the air.

About half an hour before, my sister, father, and I had lifted the sheet upon which my mother had lain since her death the day before, and using it like a sling carried her body to her coffin, which had been brought in from the garage—where it, along with my father's, had been waiting for two years—to the living room. Her frail-looking body was heavier than I'd expected. The coffin, made of hewn pine, was a thing of beauty; its beveled edges reflected both simplicity and an attention to craftsmanship. Its lid, the underside of which my father had joked about taping a picture of himself to, so that mom could see him when she was "down there," fit with a satisfying snugness. Even so, the handles on the sides hadn't been positioned with regard to weight distribution: the frontmost left side rail, which I was responsible for holding, and which should have been placed closer to the front, had been positioned closer to the coffin's midsection.

I'd wrapped a rope that had been tied to this rail around my hand and, with the other three men who'd been charged with lowering my mother's coffin into her grave, dug the day before by friends of my father, pulled upwards and edged toward the hole.

As we began to lower it, the whole thing tilted ominously forward. My cousin's husband, who happened to be standing at the head of the grave, jumped inside to support the coffin at the last minute and prevent it from falling headlong into the hole.

I'd anchored the rope around my middle finger, which meant that it—this sole finger—was bearing all the weight for which I was responsible. I imagined the rope yanking the finger completely off, the digit toppling onto the coffin lid, and my hand spurting blood. I managed to twist it free. The finger was ringed and grooved with a dark purple indention. I showed it to my father, who predicted that I'd have nerve damage. And I did. I was most aware of this loss of sensation—I could feel the numbness at the fingertip's center—when typing. Whenever I hit the number 3, say, or the letters E, D, or C. I could ignore it but it was difficult. E was, after all, the most used letter in the English language. You couldn't spell "mother" or "love" or "finger" or "dead" or "cemetery" without it.

Had my mother known the weight of her dead body would've nearly ripped off one of my fingers, she would have laughed. Not because she was unkind but because that's how she reacted to the life's absurdities: with laughter. And despite the sadness and confusion that often attended the slow erasure of her mind, she never fell into a darkness so low that she couldn't be lit up, if only momentarily, by humor. In the years preceding her death, whenever I called my parents—I always called their landline due to the spotty cell service that deep in the mountains—my father would answer, and then activate the speakerphone, so that my mother could hear; though in her final years she contributed little to the conversations, except to punctuate the dialogues between my father and me by unleashing one of her many exclamations—"that's right!" to affirm, or "huh-uh!" as an expression of disbelief

Or, she laughed.

"Who's that cackling in the background?" I'd say, and my father might make a joke about having purchased a new chicken, or claim that Buster—the African gray parrot who could imitate the microwave beep, sing the first few notes of the "Star Spangled Banner," and laugh like my mother—had come back to visit.

That one person could draw from such a vast repertoire of sounds when laughing—the air-compressor wheeze, the explosive guffaw, the hoot, the *whoo-hoo-hoo*, the *lu-lu-ha*, the *hee-hee-hee*, the silent body tremble, the throw-your-head-back-with-abandon-and-howl—was amazing, but occasionally, especially during the sullen years of my adolescence, my mother's laughter proved irritating, since the majority of these laughs arrived with a frequency unmatched by any other human being I'd ever met. *I mean, come on, Mom,* I often said to her. *What's so funny?* Do she really have *that* much to laugh about? Did every phone call really occasion such unabashed hilarity?

"Well," she would say, whenever I called her relentless glee into question, "would you rather have a mean mama?"

I'd roll my eyes, and mock one of her laughs, as I had learned, over the years, to reproduce each one with a near-perfect fidelity, the act of which only served to re-ignite her laughter; that is, my imitation of her laugh gave birth to a different laugh, and I'd reproduce *that* laugh, and she'd respond with another kind of laugh, and I'd imitate that one. We would produce a cycle of real laugh, echo laugh, real laugh, echo laugh, moving through each version until we came full circle and one of us—usually I was the one who surrendered—came to our senses and stopped.

My mother didn't mind when my sister or I made fun of her. Or when my father, always the one playful antagonist, gave her a hard time. She loved a good joke, especially at her own expense. She'd also been something of a comeback queen. Granted, her exclamations were limited to a number of catch phrases—"Double ditto" if she agreed; "I think not!" if she didn't; "Ew! I wouldn't want that in my brain bank!" if she were to encounter a sight or idea she found distasteful; "Heavens!" when dismayed; "I swannee" when confounded, "oh, brother" or "For pity's sake" if somebody had gone too far—but she fired each of them off with a confidence and authority that suggested she could take as much as you could give.

I can only remember my mother crying on three different occasions before she got sick. She cried when a fellow church member called her "stuck up." She cried the day I left to drive by myself across the country to Yellowstone National Park, where I had secured a job bussing tables at the Old Faithful Inn. And she cried during the conversation I had with her, over the telephone, about my first book—a collection of stories—which happened to be the same year, as it turned out, that we noticed that mom seemed to be repeating things more often and losing track of her keys. A couple months after the book came out, I received an email from one of my cousins. She'd written me because she'd read an interview with me, in which I'd been asked what my parents thought about my stories. I claimed not to know. That my mother always said something positive, like, "What an imagination you have!" And that my father wasn't a reader, per se. More of an internet browser and Sudoku player. In her email, my cousin assured me that this wasn't the case. The truth was that my parents had not liked what I'd written. That my portrayal of their church, fictional members of which had appeared in three of my eleven stories, had not been accurate or fair. "It's like listening to someone telling lies about people you love," my father had reportedly said. Furthermore, according to my cousin, my parents had been heartbroken. They were "terrified for my soul." And that people in my family were terrified to talk to me about religion, for fear that they'd push me further away from "the truth." But they—and she—loved me so much. Therefore, she couldn't let me slide away without a fight.

A few hours after receiving my cousin's email, and writing a haughty reply, I dialed my parents' landline. My mother picked up.

"Wanna hear something crazy?" I said.

She laughed. Of course she would.

I summarized my cousin's letter as succinctly as possible. "Apparently," I added, "you're 'heartbroken' and 'terrified for my soul.'"

I expected utter dismay. Absolute denial. Assurance that my cousin had exaggerated, misremembered, or simply *lied*.

The resultant silence was sudden and deep. For a second, I thought we'd been disconnected.

"Hello?" I said.

Silence.

"Mom?" I said. "You there?"

She sniffed. Emitted a weepy moan.

"Mom," I said, my own eyes watering. "What's wrong?"

"Oh," she replied, gasping loudly, as if she'd emerged from having swum a long distance underwater. "I just want us all to be together in the end."

I opened my mouth. No words came.

I knew that when my mother had said, "I just want us all to be together in the end," that by "the end" she'd meant "heaven."

And that by "us" she'd meant "our family."

And that "our family" had meant "everyone else." And that she was imagining heaven without me, and that was making her sad.

I knew she believed that only God could truly know the contents of a person's heart, and so I reminded her of this. I knew she believed that only God knew who would end up in heaven, and that people who appeared to be living holy lives on earth right now might not make it, and I reminded her of this, too. I told her not to worry about me, and that just because my sister went to church every Saturday, didn't mean she should worry about her any less. In other words, I tried to console her. And she appeared, for the time being, to be consoled. But I have no way of knowing if she ever came to terms with what I'd written, because after this conversation, I never brought up the subject of my writing with her again. In less than a year, the Great Forgetting would begin. My family members would begin to notice that my mother had a habit of repeating herself. She'd embark on long searches for things that she'd lost. She'd go to the grocery store and buy duplicates of things in her refrigerator that had already been duplicated. She would bake pies without essential ingredients. Ten years later, I'd be wrapping my hand with a rope whose other end was tied in a knot around the handle of her coffin, which four other members of my family were lowering into a freshly dug grave. Whether that broken heart of hers had ever been mended, or if she had ever surrendered the anxiety she had about my eternal salvation to heaven, will remain a secret I expect never to unlock.

I'd broken the finger whose tip was now dead, along with my ring and pinky, in Oregon late summer of 1996, when the dune buggy I'd been driving flipped over. Despite having been instructed, in the event of a crash, not to grab onto the crash bar, that's exactly what I'd done. Afterward, I stared in shock at the result: grimy with sand and blood, my mangled hand revealed crushed bone fragments and bloody tissue. My friend Susannah, who kept muttering *oh my God*, drove me to the hospital, which happened to be no more than a quarter mile up the road. There, in the ER, a doctor injected the hand with a numbing agent. The pressure made me think it was about to explode. I wrongly supposed I'd never have full use of the hand to do things like play guitar again.

I'd spent that summer waiting tables at the Old Faithful Inn, ferrying platters of crusted trout and ribeyes to hungry, impatient tourists. After my shifts, I jogged along moonlit boardwalks, inhaling geyser steam that smelled like rotten eggs. In September, not long after the first snowflakes began crashing into the windows of the Inn's restaurant, Susannah arrived, and I said goodbye to my friends and she and I drove through Glacier National Park to Seattle and Portland. I left Oregon shortly after my accident in the dunes, my arm wrapped in tape, a bottle of hydrocodone pills in the pocket of my cargo shorts and D. J. Shadow's just-released *Entroducing* blaring from my Nissan Maxima's CD player. Susannah and I snorted crushed Ritalin through McDonald's straws from the cover of a Led Zeppelin boxed set. We took pulls of Jack Daniel's, stopped to photograph banana slugs and ancient trees shrouded in fog in the Redwood National Park. In L. A., we visited the Getty museum. Crossed the border in Mexico, took a boat-like cab that lunged through the streets to a pharmacy. Recrossed the border with pills in our shoes. Got stopped at a border control just outside White Sands, where dunes drifted like bright frozen waves. The border patrol officer asked if he could search the vehicle. We had the aforementioned pills, an open bottle of whiskey, a baggy of marijuana shake. We would've been busted if not for the bike and bike rack strapped to the trunk. The officer hadn't wanted to fool with removing it. Or, he hadn't wanted to fool with us, two young white people wrongly presumed innocent of drug smuggling. He waved us on. I never told my mother about this close call. She would have expressed disbelief had I ever tried. She didn't like to imagine that her baby would ever have been capable of doing those kinds of things. Maybe because she was too busy praying, in Jesus's holy name, for my salvation.

In direct opposition to my parents' wishes, and maybe as a kind of experiment, I liked to think I was raising my son without religion. I say "religion" but I guess what I actually mean is: We never indoctrinated him into any particular belief system, at least not with anything resembling vigor or consistency. Yes, we had him baptized as a baby into the Epsicopal church—an event my mother seemed to deny was happening, as she'd kept referring to the event as his "dedication," which happens to be the word Adventists use when publicly committing their infants to the care of the Lord. For a while, we took him to Sunday School at our local Episcopal church, and shamed him for his inability to sit still during sermons, but we never enforced him to pledge allegiance to any specific beliefs. I was much more interested in bribing him to read Alan Watt's *On the Taboo of Knowing Who You Are* or, once he'd graduated high school, giving him a copy of the *Tao Te Ching*, and telling him that if he ever needed to chill out he should read it. In fact, had anyone ever quizzed him about the specifics of Adventism, he could have told you maybe three things about it: it was the denomination to which Grandmama and Papaw belonged, they went to church on Saturdays, and they didn't eat bacon. It baffled me sometimes to realize how little he knew about Adventism—I guess part of me expected he'd just absorb it via osmosis—and how easy it was for him to forget so many things I'd told him about the deprivations of my own childhood.

"I've been going through her old cookbooks," my sister said. "I had this strange feeling that I was going to find a message from her somewhere. I know it sounds crazy. But I couldn't help it. Like I kept turning pages, nursing this strange hopefulness that she'd a little note tucked somewhere. Like a secret. Just for me."

I knew exactly what she meant. After all, once upon a

time, our mother had been a writer. That is, she regularly put pen to paper, and she did so for utterly pragmatic reasons: daily notes to my sister and me in our lunchboxes, cards to friends on their birthdays, frequent correspondence with her friends from boarding school and college, notes on calendars, grocery lists, phone numbers, and bible verses she copied into notebooks for inspirational purposes. Then there was the little book that lived in a drawer in my mother's bedside table, whose cover featured one of the wide-eyed waifs that made Betsey Clark, an artist who made a living drawing adorable urchins for Hallmark in the 1970s, a household name. A phrase hovered above the cartoon child: "Remembered joys are never past."

The book opens in present tense, with the following line: "At 12:28 today, I hear my baby cry for the first time." How my mother had the presence of mind or physical wherewithal to make an entry in this book the day she gave birth for the first time is something of a mystery. Furthermore, there is not a single mistake or strikethrough—not on this page, or any other. From October to December 31, 1974, thirty-eight entries appear. The book chronicles observations ("Your upper laterals look like fangs"), boring everyday details ("You were really fussy this afternoon. I finally gave you some aspirin"), personal milestones ("You like adult food now!"), idiosyncrasies ("You entertained everyone at the Dr's office—you shake your head 'no' all the time, think you're a real big shot"), things to "work on" ("Always reaching and grabbing for something. Usually things that are a 'no-no'!"), and modes of punishment ("have started to use the spatula for spankings").

Despite the effusive nature of the book—my mother's favorite punctuation mark, in both this ledger and in all forms of correspondence, was the exclamation point—the majority of the entries are not, as it turns out, very interesting. It is difficult, perhaps, to make the everyday lives of babies and very young children interesting to anybody but the person documenting them. Even so, at the time, it was interesting to *me*. The book could tell me things about myself I didn't know, had cataloged things I'd done that I had no memory of. "You love to look at yourself in the mirror," my mother wrote. And I guess it was true, in more ways than one; after all, I kept coming back to this book, a different kind of mirror than the one in the bathroom I shared with my sister. I'd forget the little diary existed, catch sight of it or suddenly remember, and pay it a visit, hoping that a section had been added. And often it had.

This book, my mother once explained, would one day be given to my future wife, who, she seemed to think, would be so crazy about me that she'd want to devour every possible detail of my life. Odd, then, that the book itself would be written in second person, addressed, not to an unnamed woman, but to me.

I'd been taught as a child that I was being observed at all times by supernatural entities. I was being watched, of course, by God, who created, sustained, and supervised the earth. I was being watched by my guardian angel, who, once his identity was revealed to me in heaven, would tell me about all the times that I had, thanks to divine intervention, unwittingly avoided danger and cheated death. I was likely also being watched by any number of evil angels and possibly, on occasion, by Satan himself. There were, I knew, other worlds with other beings, who, unlike humans, had passed their own Gardens-of-Eden tests, had not eaten from their Trees of Knowledge of Good and Evil, and had therefore not fallen from perfection, and that these righteous aliens were watching our earthly drama unfold. And then there was my recording angel.

The job of a recording angel was to record the deeds of whatever human they had been given charge to observe: every action, good or bad. Once this earthly subject had expelled its last breath, the book would be delivered to the Most Holy Place in the Heavenly Sanctuary, where Jesus Christ would blot out with his blood the sins of the redeemed, and mark as lost those who had not asked for forgiveness.

I didn't know what happened to the books after Jesus had read them. I don't remember thinking much about the details of how this particular heavenly drama might unfold, and in fact didn't think about it much at all, except on the occasions when ministers pointed out that this ministry of Jesus on behalf of all humanity was going on right now. I didn't wonder how my recording angel was able to watch me from such a great distance, if he or she or it had some kind of magical telescope, or if this angel stared at a screen or a TV that played a single channel dedicated of my unfolding life, or had simply been granted a superior vision—perhaps, like Superman, all creatures of the universe who had not fallen from their original state could zoom in on anything in the universe, no matter how far away. I didn't wonder if the books waiting to be read by Jesus were on some kind of conveyor belt, or if the ones Jesus had finished reading were stored in two different libraries—SAVED and DOOMED—or if they had been delivered to a holy courtroom where Jesus, as humanity's advocate and defense lawyer, argued against Satan, the prosecutor, on behalf of the forgiven. I didn't wonder if the blood Jesus used was real or metaphorical, if he dabbed a finger into the seeping wound of his other hand—or, more likely, wrists, as I knew or had been told that the weight of his body, however slight, would have caused the nails to rip through his palms if the Roman guards had nailed him to the cross in that manner, which meant it was more likely that they'd drive them through the radial nerves of his wrists—like a scribe dipping a quill into an inkwell, and blotting out certain descriptions of whatever wrongs I'd committed. I didn't think about these things because whenever I thought about this so-called Investigative Judgment, I couldn't help wondering how many times I'd sinned without knowing it. What if I'd slipped up and forgotten to ask forgiveness? Or even worse: What if I'd done something that I'd known was wrong, and assumed could be forgiven after? Could such a thing be erased? And where did those bad things go when they died?

Recently, Kelly disposed of the journals she'd kept during her adolescence and early twenties. She had an entire plastic tub of them she stored under the guest bedroom bed. I'd never read them but often imagined—and hoped—that someday I might be allowed and so this news disappointed me. I couldn't imagine throwing such valuable personal history away. Who knew what forgotten treasures might be lying inside? Kelly shrugged. The journals had served their purpose—had given her a void in which to scream the things she couldn't talk about during the ten years she'd spent actively grieving her mother's death, of breast cancer, at forty-six. Kelly had been fourteen at the time: a broken-hearted teenager who'd be forced to navigate high school while living with an alcoholic father. Now, she didn't need keepsakes of a time she had no desire to revisit. I, on the other hand, had kept every diary and journal I'd ever had, a stack of ephemera that included sketch pads from my adolescence, college notebooks, and every single letter that any girl had sent me during boarding school, when, every Sunday night, during an event called "Pony Express," boys and girls would exchange handwritten notes. I keep a giant box of those letters—some of which are intricately folded—in the storage room in our basement. I rarely if ever look at them but for some reason I can't bring myself to throw them away. The only letters I tossed, without thinking, into the garbage had been written to me by my mother. An avid correspondent, she frequently sent care packages during my four years at boarding school: heart-shaped brownies, chocolate chip cookies, boxes of fruit juice, granola bars, individual packages of crackers that came with little tubs of artificial cheese and a tiny plastic wand for spreading. And notes. Quickly jotted messages on cards or stationery describing what her day had been like. The weather. A report about what my father was up to: mowing the lawn, cutting wood, scraping the gravel drive with his tractor. I never considered preserving these messages. It was *just Mom*, after all. She had an entire reservoir of material inside her that I could access whenever I wanted. I threw almost every one of her letters into the trash after reading them. I have but a few. I would in a heartbeat trade all the other letters for the ones of my mom's I discarded.

Now, the only letter I own is a postcard she'd included with a birthday check, four years before she died. On the card, she'd written *Hi sweet ones! We are wishing we were closer! Sorry to be so late! Love you all—wish we could live by each other all the time.* X.O.X.O. I remember that I'd been surprised, upon having received this awkwardly phrased and somewhat repetitive message, that she still had the wherewithal to write anything at all. The handwriting is wobbly and the two hearts she'd drawn appeared bloated and wonky, as if she'd had trouble working the pen. The only message from my mother that I held onto, as it turned out, was the very last one she'd ever sent.

When I was at boarding school, my father never wrote me any letters. Or, rather, he never sent the letters he wrote. I found some, once, when I was rummaging through his dresser, searching for a shirt to borrow. I was surprised to find, between two folded sweaters, several notebook pages upon which his handwriting appeared. This letter articulated particular concerns, namely those of the rock and roll variety. My father had gone into my bedroom for some reason, and had taken a moment to inventory a stack of CDs sitting next to my stereo. In the letter, he said that he'd known I'd been listening to rock music, but he'd been surprised to see the band Guns N' Roses, as he seemed to remember me saying that I wasn't a fan of "the harder stuff." I can't remember what else the letter said, except maybe to express concern about the influence of secular rock music upon a young Christian's mind—not to mention their eternal soul—but years later I did bring up the fact that he'd written to me and never sent them. "I've written you several letters over the years," he admitted.

"Why didn't you send them?" I asked.

"Because," he said, "I actually think I wrote them more for me."

"I'm worried about Dad," my sister Carrie said. It was the end of the first week of March. She'd called me from the kitchen of her house in Tennessee, about thirty minutes east of Knoxville, a town whose name always summoned the golden sun sphere poised on its tower and the World's Fair we attended back in 1982, where, for a few panic-stricken minutes, my sister had gotten lost in the crowds.

"Why?" I said.

"I just don't like to think of him up there all alone. Coming home after work to that big dark house. It makes me sad." Now Carrie lived in a big Victorian house with an iron fence around it. The house had once belonged to a doctor who'd practiced on the first floor. One of the rooms, with built in cubbies and shelves and drawers in the walls, had served as a small pharmacy. On the second floor: bedrooms and my brother-in-law's office, which in addition to three computer screens in a corner of the room included a fish tank and terrariums for his five tortoises, bearded lizard, and boa constrictor. Their house was full of life, as my parents' house had once been.

"He likes being by himself."

"Not all the time."

"He has the lights to keep him company."

"That's what I'm talking about. Also, I don't like the lights."

"Why not?"

"I don't want him to be scared."

"What's to be scared of?"

"He doesn't know what they are. It's bothering him."

For weeks I'd been calling my father every day to ask what

he'd seen the night before. Every night, my father would wake and sit up to pee into his Mason jar. Afterwards, he'd peer out his window. Some nights the lights were active. Other nights? Not so much. Some nights, my father said, it would be rare for a minute to go by without seeing one— that is, unless he got out his phone. Then they'd stop altogether. Sometimes, the intensity would be very bright. Other nights, they'd be very faint. Sometimes the lights were white. Sometimes they were red, yellow. One night, a light had swooped upward. That, he'd said, had been strange. He'd never seen them move before. But after all this time, he hadn't said anything to me about being afraid. He'd never said anything about how the lights had made him feel. Why hadn't it occurred to me to ask?

My mother liked to crank up her soft South Carolina drawl. She had a weakness for suddenly distorted facial expressions. She could touch the tip of her nose with her tongue. She struck overly dramatic poses. She pretended to dance by biting her lower lip, snapping her fingers, and flapping her arms. She did not like cupboards that had been left open. She wasn't a fan of houseflies, indoor pets, dirty carpets, slow drivers, rap music, rock and roll, profanity, spicy food, or Willie Nelson's braids. She relished vigorous walks and insisted on using her Nordic hiking poles to flick sticks off the road. She needed her paths to be free and clear and clean. She needed chocolate and cake and ice cream and oranges and blisteringly hot cups of Maxwell House International Café instant coffee. She claimed, preposterously, to be immune to caffeine. Over the course of her life, she ate an estimated 15,000 slabs of peanut-butter-and-applesauce toast. She loved children and babies and dolls and tea parties and playing pretend. She watched *The Sound of Music* an estimated fifty-three times. She adored the Swiss Alps. She began every day with her open bible. She learned to paint, but once the walls of our house had been sufficiently decorated, she laid down her brush. She sewed only to clothe herself and my sister. She took photographs to document things she wanted us all to remember: her children making silly faces in bathtubs, sledding on snowy days, my father holding an opossum by the tail. She wrote entire books, only to record significant family narratives, so that my sister and I could reflect on our childhoods as adults.

My mother's sickness had announced itself, rather unceremoniously, with the simple act of forgetting. With the people my mother loved no longer being able to deny that she was constantly repeating herself. To leaving out key ingredients in the pies she was making. To not being able to use her phone to take pictures or make calls. To studying a once-familiar recipe and collapsing into sorrow with the realization that, in her own words, she couldn't do anything anymore. In the end, she literally could only sleep and breathe on her own.

One night not too long before she died, my father and our friend Judy—a woman who had always been beloved by our family for her frank and straightforward opinions as well as her sense of humor—helped get my mother ready for bed: brushed her teeth, put her into her pajamas, helped her onto and off of the toilet. I went in to say goodnight. My mother lay on her back, the covers pulled up to her chin. Her expression was one of sickening discomfort. Eyes squinted shut, brow deeply furrowed, lips pursed.

My father patted her leg and said, "Okay, now it's my turn for Judy to wipe *me*!" And my mother, who had looked like she'd been trying to shut the world out, opened her eyes wide and erupted into laughter. And until the day she died, no matter how bad things got, no matter how sad she became, those she loved could still summon her smile and laugh. In the right moment, the right someone could say something that tickled her, or my father, at work, might use an app to check the cameras he'd positioned all throughout the house and find mom wandering around in a shirt and underwear, and then call her up to ask her why she was walking around without pants, and that old familiar brightness—my mother's inexhaustible laughter—would burst through like a laser beam of sunlight slicing through the world's darkest storm cloud.

IX. GOING VIRAL

What day was it? Couldn't remember. Furthermore: who cared? Once the pandemic hit the States and the Virginia governor had decreed a lockdown, it became impossible to account, with any accuracy, for the passage of time. I went days—and then an entire week—without talking to my father. I hadn't forgotten about the lights, but I'd stopped calling him every morning to record his observations, and I'd lost track of the little orange journal I'd been using to scribble notes in during those daily calls. Couldn't find the where-withal to look for it. It seemed as if nobody could say or type in an email or text message the word *time* without using the modifiers *dark* or *uncertain*. Instead of researching ghost lights, I spent hours trolling Amazon, asking myself questions like: "Should I buy an ultraviolet wand sanitizer? A generator? A case of beef jerky? Canned soup?" I'd already purchased an emergency food bucket (which no UPS delivery person would ever deliver), three metal COVID keys (for hooking door handles and pressing buttons I wanted to avoid touching), two digital thermometers, 80 NAHU Ear Thermometer Probe Covers, a box of Idahoan Italian Sausage and Potato Hearty Soup (made with gluten-free, 100-percent Idaho potatoes), a Zacurate Pro Series 500DL Fingertip Pulse Oximeter Blood Oxygen Saturation Monitor with Silicone Cover (batteries and lanyard included), a

Voldyne 5000 Volumetric Exerciser, and rolls of toilet paper that I'd forget I'd ever ordered. Three months later, they'd show up, in packaging embossed with letters from an alphabet whose country of origin I couldn't identify.

I was, as many were in the beginning weeks and months of the pandemic, afraid. I did not want to get sick. I preferred not to suffer. I would rather avoid any and all situations wherein suffocation played a role in my demise. Was I naïve for thinking that I, as a relatively young and healthy person, would maybe like to go ahead and get the virus? Was it really going to take a year—or two—for scientists to develop a vaccine? Was COVID here...to *stay*? The only thing I could really say for sure, was this: I was one of the lucky ones. I wasn't a worker whose occupation had been deemed "essential." I wasn't on the front lines. I didn't have to deliver groceries. I wasn't pulling sixty-hour weeks at a hospital. I wasn't stacking bodies in refrigerated trucks. I was a middle-aged white man living in a college town on a verdant plateau in southern Appalachia. I had a decent-paying job that allowed—insisted, in fact—that I work remotely, and because I enjoyed a great deal of autonomy, and because the idea of teaching on Zoom filled me with the kind of existential dread that would cause me to break out into a sweat, I'd elected to teach my courses asynchronously. I had a house and a fenced-in backyard and a pair of cats who, during certain parts of the day, enjoyed my affections. My wife—a woman I'd been married to for over twenty years, and who served as the associate chair of our English department—was the smartest and also the most fun person I knew. My son would soon gain acceptance into an architecture program at the university he most wanted to attend. I needed not to fear the police. I took walks in a neighborhood without any thought for my safety. I had an extra refrigerator in my garage. I had a *garage*.

Elsewhere, according to my phone, into which I stared for hours, things looked... not so great.

According to *New Scientist*, researchers believed that they might've discovered a parallel universe going backward in time and that "strange particles observed by an experiment in Antarctica could be evidence of an alternative reality where everything [was] upside down."

On TikTok, two males narrated their removal from a Walmart, thanks to a cop who'd ordered them to leave the store—ostensibly because they had been wearing protective surgical masks.

A white man proudly proclaimed he didn't believe that the coronavirus was real. And that he never washed his hands. And that pretty much all the conspiracies were true. 9/11 was an inside job. Vaccines were poison. No human had walked on the moon. The man yelling these things claimed he'd been eating raw meat and uncooked eggs for years. And that nothing bad ever happened to him. And that nothing ever would.

"Cough in my face!" he commanded, to no one in particular, but also: to everyone.

And then someone did.

And then the man laughed.

He was insane! A lunatic. Right?

I hearted the video. Not because I actually liked it. Because I couldn't believe what I was seeing. And because I knew, therefore, that I'd want to see it again.

I had resolved, at the beginning of 2020, to walk five miles a day. Once quarantine began, it seemed like the thing a lot of people I knew were doing to "stay sane." Pressing pause on whatever I was doing—reading assignments, posting announcements to class, scrolling through TikTok, writing a quarantine journal to preserve the bizarre events of the pandemic—and taking a walk was, in many ways, like refreshing the screen of my brain. I downloaded the lectures of Alan Watts to distract me from the idea that the virus sweeping the planet might very well cause society as we knew it to completely crumble. Watt's raspy voice, his British accent, the way he broke suddenly into crackling laughter: I found it all quite soothing. Plus, I liked entertaining his ideas; in a world of uncertainties and delusions, his descriptions of reality seemed irrefutable. According to Watts, one of the earth's functions was "to people." The earth "peopled." It flowered. Fruited. Buffaloed. Fished. Monkeyed. Snaked. Now, it was virusing. All these things were *symptoms* of Earth. Furthermore: the universe was one singular massively long event. The only constant? Change.

All over the world, people who were not me were dying. My mom had missed this historic event and I didn't know if I should feel grateful. I imagined her body, in a coffin six feet below the mound of moss and flowers that her grandchildren and grand-nieces and nephews had gathered and assembled there, and which acted as a kind of luminous crown for her grave. Presumably, down there in the dark, her body had long since bloated and begun to liquefy. From what I'd read online about the deterioration of the buried dead, it was quite possible that the pressure of gasses being released had caused the coffin to crack and liquids to breach. I imagined the withered bouquet of flowers in her fist turning to dust. My mother's skin by now might have blackened and shrunk, outlining the shape of her bones. I imagined underground scavengers feasting on the banquet that was her putrefaction. The disintegration of her pajamas. Tissue collapsing to slush. Teeth falling out of the skull. Fat turning to so-called "grave wax." Somehow, imagining this process was comforting. My mother's body was, in a sense, alive with all these various energies, playing its part in the only eternity we could verify for sure: relentless transformation.

The videos I'd recorded of the blinking light that Lil Evan and I had watched lived an afterlife on my phone. Every few days, I'd open the photo app and scroll backwards, past images of sunsets and backyard dinner parties and cats napping and street lamps igniting blooming dogwoods to re-watch them. Aside from a deep, abiding blackness, there was never anything to see. I could hear the creek. I could hear Lil Evan saying, "there" and "there" and "again" and "again" and me saying, "wow" and "yep" and "damn." I watched the videos anyway. Maybe, I told myself, I'd missed something during previous viewings. Maybe the saved movies needed time to develop. To incubate. Or something.

I know how it sounds.

I thought it just the same.

My mother's death. The lights. COVID-19. Great calamities. The fact that we had elected a toxic blowhard to be our president and who was now endorsing horse deworming pills as treatment for the virus and suggesting we might inject "something like" Clorox into our bloodstreams. All the anti-mask people. The COVID deniers. One event seemed to precede another. But now time had slowed down and sped up and it could feel, in the right moment, as if everything was happening at once—or not at all. My mother was still alive but dead. The lights had appeared but had gone out. COVID-19 was everywhere and nowhere. And though I always seemed to be walking, I always ended up back at my house, where I started, which made it feel I'd never really gone anywhere.

I composed an announcement regarding the now-asynchronous nature of our course for the graduate students in my "Form & Theory of Fiction" class. *I hope you all are well,* I wrote. *Me? I'm a ghost haunting my former life. A glitchy NPC in an abandoned video game. A dysfunctional node on the universe's antennae. How are you guys maintaining sanity? I'd love to hear about it. As for myself, I've been walking a lot, tending to my lawn, talking on the phone, and trying to convince my cats they don't have to practice social distancing.*

One student—a friendly, overachieving go-getter, with a penchant for wearing vests and bow ties—responded: *Wow, These announcements are great.*

From everyone else: absolutely nothing.

In the throes of the inexplicable, my thinking, like so many others, seemed especially vulnerable to the entertaining of preposterous notions. Had the blinking lights in the woods been some kind of warning...about COVID? Had they represented a glitch in the simulation? A signal from an otherworldly observer? A divine harbinger? Any possible analysis seemed worthy of consideration. And so, I climbed aboard an endlessly rotating carousel of interpretations:

Dude, that's your mom...

The lights might be alien presences...

Positive affirmation of the goodness of what's to come...

Are you open to this experience? Because there's nothing going to separate you from the light once that window's open...

Your mom was a light beam generator...

She's ready to open up her soul, her being to source...

I think it's a test...

Light is the best thing there is...

Impossible to understand...

They all sounded plausible. What if they were all somehow true?

I know how it sounds.

I thought it just the same.

"Life is a weird thing," my student Lexi wrote, in an online forum for my creative nonfiction course. "I was walking across the drill field yesterday and all I could think about was the fact that after I'm dead, this school will still be bustling with life as it has been for years and years. We are born, we live, then we die. That's it. That is our existence. We are nothing but our collective experiences and memories, all of which are gone as soon as we take our last breath. We are nothing but the people we love and the people who love us, all of which are gone when *they* take their last breaths. And eventually, there will be no trace of us. Dust in the wind. So, why? What is the point of it all? What is the point of striving for money and fame and success if it will disappear as soon as we leave the earth? Why stress? Why feel sadness? Why seek out power? It is all fleeting. And we can't stop time. That is the scariest part. Time. It is always moving, and we can't stop it. Ticking ticking ticking closer to our inevitable deaths. There's nothing to be done. Death will always win. Why does life try if death always wins? We keep looking to the future, searching for some answer to a question that doesn't exist, and sooner than later we are staring straight at death. All we have is now."

All we have is now.

I couldn't help but agree.

Alan Watts would too.

But what even was now?

Or when?

Mimi texted me a video. In it, a curve of purplish light danced against the wooded hill outside of my grandmother's house. The camera wasn't moving. The light—a curving bubble—pulsed. Expanded and contracted, like a phantasmagoric jellyfish.

I called her up.

"I was singing a thank you song to the guardians of the forest," Mimi explained, over the phone. "'Thank you, spirits!' I was singing. I wanted them to know I was grateful for their presence and protection. And then this light appeared."

I didn't ask who the guardians of the forest were.

"Lights?" I said instead. "In the *daytime?*"

"Absolutely," Mimi said.

I stared at my phone. Replayed the video. It was easy to think that what I was seeing represented a mere trick of the light. A conspiracy of sorts. The refraction that happens when you turn your phone or a camera lens toward the sun and tilt it back and forth. But the phone wasn't moving. Mimi had held it perfectly still.

"Isn't it beautiful?" she said.

Yes, I said. And I suppose in a way it was.

What I didn't say, but thought to myself: *I don't believe this is real.*

What I also didn't say, but thought to myself: *I don't know what "real" is anymore.*

Then again: did I ever?

Did the cove where my parents had built their home represent a kind of unique microclimate? Did the geology there represent a space that might act like a gargantuan light powering battery, as some scientists, who had been studying the Hessdalen lights in Norway, where luminous phenomena had been inexplicably appearing since the 1930s, supposed? Or was it, like Luisa said, my mother's spirit, briefly inhabiting a trans-dimensional space of liminality before she zoomed into the afterlife? How could I know for sure—and what did it matter if I did?

On the evening of March 13, 1997, thousands of people in and around Phoenix, Arizona claimed to see mysterious lights flying across the skies. According to Wikipedia, the "Phoenix Lights" or "Lights over Phoenix" consisted of a UFO that resembled a "carpenter's square" containing five spherical lights or possibly light-emitting engines. Among the people who claimed to have seen the incident was the governor of Arizona at the time, a one Fife Symington, who claimed that the event was "otherworldly."

I'd been tempted to use that word myself. But I hadn't

gone anywhere other than earth to see them. In fact, I'd been to the place I'd known better than any other: home.

"So," I said, to anyone who would listen. "My dad calls me on December twenty-first to say, 'Some weird stuff's been happening.' Oh wait. I already told you? Yeah. No. Okay. Yeah. Sorry. No. There's actually nothing else to report."

By the end of March, I'd told the story so much that I couldn't keep track of who I'd told and who I hadn't. And, on the rare occasions when a friend said that they hadn't heard about the lights, I'd ask them how much time they had. And then I'd happily relaunch the story, always beginning at what I had insisted, to nobody but myself, was the beginning: that night, the longest of the year, when I'd called my father and the first thing he'd said was: "Well, some weird stuff's been happening."

As it turned out, according to CBS Los Angeles, reports of paranormal activity were on the rise during lockdown. In a *New York Times* article titled "Quarantining with a Ghost? It's Scary," Molly Fitzpatrick shared stories about various people who, while quarantining, experienced unexplained phenomena: doorknobs rattling, footsteps on stairs, a white man in a World War II–era military uniform sitting at a kitchen table at 3 a.m. John E.L. Tenney, a self-described paranormal researcher and former host of the TV show *Ghost Stalkers*, estimated that he received two to five reports of a haunted house each month in 2019. In 2020, that number leapt to five to ten weekly. He'd seen spikes like this before: in 1999, before Y2K, and post-9/11.

There had also been a rise in spiritualism during the 1918 influenza pandemic. According to the History Channel website, the beloved author Arthur Conan Doyle, who lost his son Kingsley, claimed to have contacted his son during a 1919 séance. It was, Kingsley claimed, "the supreme moment of my spiritual experience."

"A large, strong hand then rested upon my head," Doyle said. "It was gently bent forward, and I felt and heard a kiss just above my brow. 'Tell me, dear, are you happy?' I cried. There was silence, and I feared he was gone. Then on a sighing note came the words, 'Yes, I am so happy.'" Later, Doyle informed a reporter that, "I have many times spoken with my son," and that he remained happy. "You see, a so-called dead man goes to a happier plane," Doyle explained. "There is no crime, no sordidness, and it is many, many times happier."

On Canvas, my students shared stories they'd written: a guide to being depressed as a freshman, a narrative that included the etymology of the word *speculum* and a scene in which the narrator ran into her rapist at a church service, and a story in fragments about a mother with cancer. Outside, the sky was full of fat, puffy clouds. No contrails. No planes. I opened my Alan Watts app and resumed listening. Watts didn't trust the idea of what he called a "ceramic universe"—one in which things were artifacts and humans the descendants of a man that God made out of clay; he much preferred—or at least was excited by—the Hindu notion of a God who'd turned himself into the things of the world in order to forget he was God. Back home, my open computer responded with an automatic Tornado Warning, and that "*a severe thunderstorm capable of producing a tornado was located over huffman, or near mountain lake, moving at 35 mph.*" Things that could scare me just by imagining them: playing Russian roulette, walking a high wire between two skyscrapers, burning at the stake, breathing on a ventilator, and getting caught in a tornado. Outside, gray clouds churned slowly. Rain blurred distant mountains. Sirens—a particular tone I couldn't ever recall having heard before—sounded alarm. Neighbors emerged from their houses, waved, looked up at the sky, pointed phones at the darkness. I could see, in my mind's eye, the whirling column of dust and trash, and remembered when Kelly, Elijah, and I were living in Iowa City fifteen years before, and how a neighbor described having witnessed the tornado that devastated that town: a churning cloud of garbage. Here, the wind picked up. Wind chimes clanged. Kelly predicted, as she often did whenever the wind turned gale-force, our deaths: one of the nine Weeping Norway Spruces standing just on the other side of our property line would fall on our house and kill us. The sirens sounded again. The warning had expired. Another storm was on the way, though. I summoned a Spotify playlist of melancholy piano songs I had made last fall after the death of my mother and dialed up images of her face. How beautiful! How oblivious! And now, how lost to oblivion. Kelly, sitting in a chair in our living room, wondered why I was crying. "Mom," I said. She hugged me. A student, submitting late work, prefaced confession of lateness with the following questions: "Is time merely as we perceive, a sequence of moments which occur in linear order? Or is it as the physicist Carlo Rovelli described it, a mush of different interrelated events on some dislinear space time continuum which could only be measured relative to one another and never accurately by some external overarching metric counting the seconds, days, and years?" Outside, petals from flowering trees and small limbs and spruce branches flew through the air. Our neighbor, the one who owned all those trees, texted an apology: "Sorry about the tree debris."

Every now and again, I found myself summoning the single finest in-class writing assignment I'd ever received a few years before, which had been written by a young woman named Brooke, a bright, attentive, and otherwise cheerful student in my contemporary fiction course. I couldn't believe she'd written it in ten minutes. And, as dark as this piece of fiction was, its refusal to offer consolation brought me comfort.

"There are times," Brooke had written, "during the slow days, during the stillness, where I almost hope that some kind of tragic accident will happen to me. I will get in a car accident that wasn't my fault. I will be martyred for my faith or die trying to save my friends from a gunman at a movie theater. Maybe it's a hero complex—I feel as if my life doesn't matter unless I'm doing something heroic, and in order to fully give myself to it, it means I have to die. Of course, the person who lives inside the backboard of my brain always protests, 'No! No!' We don't actually want that, World. I apologize on her behalf!' And then they all start wrestling.

"Because the question is: what am I going to do with my long string of tomorrows. Unless things change, I don't think I want that many. If things ended early, I would feel bad for my family's questions of 'whys' but I wouldn't feel bad for me. It's an odd, caught-in-the-middle situation. I don't want to die, but if I had a gun pointed at my head, I think the few seconds before the trigger-pull would be enough for me to release the concept of the future, and maybe even say, 'Thanks for saving me.'"

What am I going to do with my long string of tomorrows.

Good question, even if it had been missing the requisite punctuation mark. Now, more than ever, I seemed to have more time on my hands. Because of my asynchronous teaching, my students and I could do classwork whenever we pleased. Which, in some cases, meant: *never*.

In the evenings, before Kelly returned from her office, where she spent most of her time, attempting to extinguish the metaphorical fires our dear colleagues in Virginia Tech's English Department seemed so fond of lighting, I found myself returning to the photographs I'd digitized from the albums my mother had assembled during her lifetime. I'd taken these photos three years before, when my father had been treated for sepsis, after becoming sick on his annual trip with the band of local men he'd befriended to the top of a mountain where they camped near a clearing known as Hooper's Bald. He'd been subsequently airlifted by helicopter and flown to Erlanger Hospital in Chattanooga, Tennessee, where he stayed for several days and made friends with all his nurses. It was the only time during my mother's illness, I shamefully realized, that I'd volunteered to take care of her on my own. We'd taken walks up and down the gravel driveway, pausing to marvel at the waterfall whose silvery cascade slid elegantly between mossy boulders. I followed her recipe for chocolate chip cookies. I watched as she ate a piece of pie, a cookie, and another piece of pie, and then said, "I did not!" when I told her what she'd just done. I

hugged her when she cried because she couldn't compre-
hend the recipe for the sugared water for the hummingbird
feeder. And I attempted a comprehensive digitization of our
family's photo albums. Easter baskets. Birthday cakes. Snow
days. Relatives sitting cross-legged before Christmas trees. I
found myself drawn to the particulars in these photos, the
things forever lost to time: a plastic Noah's ark placemat, the
kitchen wallpaper with its repeated pattern of various hand-
drawn herbs, a Halloween Spider-Man mask, cowboy boots,
a little bottle of milk whose contents appeared to disappear
when you turned it upside down, birthday presents my mom
wrapped using the leftover San Francisco trolley wallpaper
that lined my bedroom walls, my Popeye pajamas, the tennis
balls hanging inside a bra my sister wore over her shirt, my
"Inside this shirt is the most TERRIFIC kid" T-shirt, the oil
lamps we used to light during power outages and during the
blizzard when mom cooked pancakes on the wood stove in
our basement, my sky blue Smurfs lunchbox, the oversized
glasses my mother had worn on the autumn day that our
family paddled the inflatable canoe across Nantahala Lake,
the one and only time I could ever remember that we'd ever
used that particular vessel, an unspecified period of time.
Our job was simple and all-consuming: We all had grieving
to do.

Was the pandemic all bad? Apparently, it depended on how
you chose to think about it. Some people seemed to think
it was what we deserved. Shit had been going viral for years
in the virtual realm; now it had graduated to the actual.
According to an article on the website Patheos, the earth,
which, during quarantine, had been quieter than it had in

decades, needed a Sabbath. "This might be the first time since the beginning of the Industrial Age that earth is finally getting a break from the relentless activity and growth of human industrial production," Leah D. Schade wrote. "I've noted with bitter irony," she said, "that the virus is using the same tactics against the human body that humans have used against earth's body. The virus attacks the lungs, multiplying and destroying the 'respiratory tree' down to the tiniest alveoli that enable the exchange of oxygen into our bloodstream. Similarly, humans have pushed into forests and natural areas, destroying the very trees that create the oxygen we breathe." Dr. Schade, I learned, was the assistant professor of preaching and worship at Lexington Theological Seminary in Kentucky. A professional harpist, she had released a CD of original music whose title also struck me, in this age of social distancing, as ironic: *Shall We Gather*. There were photos of her online in "Biblical drag" that resembled the kind of thing someone in that movie *Midsommar* might wear. I wanted to write to her but no matter how hard I looked, I couldn't locate her email.

If there was anything I missed about belonging to the Seventh-day Adventist church, it was keeping the Sabbath: a period of rest and reflection that had, during my childhood, awaited my family and me at the end of every week. Those hallowed hours between sundown on Friday and sundown on Saturday always felt like they constituted a kind of sanctuary in time, an invisible cathedral we Adventists constructed with our hearts and minds, the feeling of which I could still summon by listening to "Borrowed Angel," the opening song of Anita Kerr's *A Sunday Serenade*, which my father often placed on the turntable of our hi-fi as the last rays of sun were leaking into the cove where our little house lived. The blank glass of the silent TV reflected our living room, where a fire blazed in the hearth. In the kitchen, a pot of lentils bubbled on the stove. Cheese danishes bloated slowly in the oven. My mother lit candles. My sister set the dining room table. Dad stoked the fire, stabbing cindery logs. Embers wafted like celestial fireflies up the flue. Another week had ended. At some point, we might sing "Day is dying in the west / Heav'n is touching earth with rest / Wait and worship while the night/Sets her evening lamps alight / Through all the sky."

There had been something magical about those evenings: the palpable sense of a restorative force at work in our lives and in our home. To stop work, turn off the TV and radio, set aside newspapers and secular magazines, and acknowledge the arrival of Sabbath rest with prayers and throat-warming songs seemed like the most natural and comforting thing in the world. The keeping of the seventh-day Sabbath was so obviously right—"Remember the seventh day to keep it holy"—you could feel it in your bones. Like so many of the things we were expected to believe and know, like acknowledging that alcohol and cigarettes were poisons to be avoided, or that dead people were just that, dead; or that no loving God would perform a miracle to torment sinners forever with hellfire, keeping the Sabbath *made sense*. And when I consider the things I miss most about being an Adventist, it is always this tableau to which I return: the nights when, as a family, we retreated from the world, and entered a time outside of time, a sacred space of quietude that foreshadowed—as we believed holy scripture indicated—the heavenly paradise our family would someday inherit, and where we would reside together for all eternity.

Even after I stopped going to church every week, I still kept—more or less—the Sabbath. Anytime I applied for a job—bussing tables at a golf course in Massachusetts, delivering meals to tables of tourists at the Old Faithful Inn in Yellowstone, working as a cashier at Barnes & Noble, and at the Record Exchange in Raleigh—I always let my managers know that, due to "religious convictions," I would be unavailable for work on Saturdays. Exodus 20:8-11—"Remember the seventh-day," etc.—might as well have been imprinted into my DNA. I might not believe that Ellen White was a true prophet, or that Seventh-day Adventists were God's chosen people, or that if you went into a movie theater your guardian angel would stand outside the door and weep, or that the necktie—as one of my fellow church members once asserted— had been devised by homosexuals as a kind of wearable napkin that gay men used to wipe their mouths after "servicing" one another, but I did believe in the Sabbath. As I was often reminded in my youth, it was the sole commandment that began with the word "remember," and the only one that the rest of Christendom seemed to have forgotten. And so it was easy to think that we Adventists were special. That we had access to what felt like secret knowledge, even though it had been spelled out, plain as day, by the Lord our God.

"So, we're seeing a lot of conspiracy theories out there right now and it's very very easy to get sucked down the rabbit hole about this stuff," TikTok user thestreamofdavid claimed. "*But* I have to tell you that the reason we're seeing all this stuff, the reason everything is happening right now on planet Earth the way that it is, is because we're experiencing a global awakening. A global reset, if you will. A disruption of planet

Earth. We have created this disruption by our questioning of all our institutions. That's why we're seeing them begin to crumble beneath our feet. Religions, governments, even law enforcement, even the monarchy—we're seeing all of that stuff begin to deteriorate because we're questioning the need for it. So, you're seeing conspiracy theories bubble up. It's okay. You're going to see things that are going to freak you out pretty soon but you're gonna adjust to that reality; it's important to understand that your vibration is the most important thing. When you keep your vibration high at a place of clarity and understanding you have the most to offer humanity from that space. When you get down into fear, you have nothing to offer anyone, so don't let it freak you out. It's fine. This is a fantastic time to be alive."

I remembered the other man. The one who demanded somebody cough in his face. Was this dude also out of his mind? Was I? Who wasn't at this point?

I had no idea.

Whatever.

I hearted this video too.

The sky continued to look empty and clean. Insects whirled through the air. Trees bloomed. According to an article on CNN, the earth was shaking less. Good news, apparently, for scientists looking through telescopes in search of extra-terrestrial life. Even so, Noam Chomsky, white-haired and haggardly bearded, concluded that our current situation was "dire."

Other people on the internet and in real life seemed to be using the phrase "End Times" more than ever. It made me wonder if Seventh-day Adventists had been talking more about the apocalypse. Even I found myself giving into the temptation to refer to pre-pandemic time as "the before times." I entered "Adventist" and "COVID" and "end times" into Google. The first hit I got was an article titled, "COVID-19: A Sign to Rethink Some Adventist Beliefs."

"COVID-19, is a wakeup call for some of these doubting Thomases," the article—no attribution had been given to its author—claimed. "Some are now rethinking Adventist doctrinal positions as we see that prophecies are coming true and now recognize the value of the principles of the doctrines. Thus, COVID-19 may not just be a sign of the times, but a sign to our own body of faith.

"Take, for example, Ellen G. White's warning of more than 100 years ago to move out of the city in the last days. She wrote that 'the cities will be filled with confusion, violence and crime, and that these things will increase till the end of this earth's history.' And again, 'When God's restraining hand is removed, the destroyer begins his work. Then in our cities the greatest calamities will come.' Furthermore, she emphasized that no city will escape the turmoil: 'The end is near and every city is to be turned upside down every way.'"

As a boy, I often felt sorry for myself because—unlike all my cousins in Greenville, South Carolina—I lived in the middle of nowhere, and was often bored out of my mind. And, supposing I had the nerve to express such complaints in the presence of my grandmother—the one who'd requested to be suffocated by a pillow were she to ever lose her mind—she'd inform me that I needed to read the chapter in *The Great Controversy* on the "Time of Trouble." This chapter, as it turned out, had been titled "The Time of Trouble" and had been written in the nineteenth century by our church prophetess, whose mission had been to portray the "conflict of the ages" between Christ and Satan, a battle that had begun in heaven during the fall of Lucifer and which would continue until the destruction of the wicked, culminating at some future date in an Earth made new. "The Time of Trouble" was the only chapter of this book I'd read in its entirety, mainly because that part was considered to be the most harrowing, since it included a detailed prophecy concerning the future tribulations that the remnant church—i.e., the Sabbath-keeping Seventh-day Adventists—would be forced to suffer at the close of "probation," when Christ, who SDAs believed had been ministering since 1844 in the heavenly sanctuary, completed the work of judging who would live forever with him in heaven, and who, after being consumed by celestial fire, would not. Once Christ had checked this off his to-do list, the forces of evil, which had heretofore been restrained by God, would be given permission to assault the earth. "In that fearful time," Mrs. White wrote, "the righteous must live in the sight of a holy God without an intercessor. The restraint which has been upon the wicked is removed, and Satan has entire control of the finally impenitent. God's long-suffering has ended. The world has rejected His mercy, despised His love, and trampled upon His law. The wicked have passed the boundary of their probation; the Spirit of God, persistently resisted, has been at last withdrawn. Unsheltered by divine grace, they have no protection from the wicked one. Satan will then plunge the inhabitants of the earth into one great, final trouble. As the angels of God cease to hold in check the fierce winds of human passion, all the elements of strife will be let loose. The whole world will be involved in ruin more terrible than that which came upon Jerusalem of old."

Had you asked me as a kid to explain how, exactly, the angels of God were holding in check "the fierce winds of human passion," I doubt that I could've have told you anything specific, though I might've imagined a group of celestial beings with arms outstretched orbiting a churning black cloud, something akin to the menacing "Nothing" from the movie *The NeverEnding Story*, with which I was more than a little acquainted. Even so, the idea of an unseen army of good angels and an unseen army of bad angels—in other words, an entire classification of invisible beings who had taken and presumably remained dedicated to their respective sides—made complete sense to me. By the time I was an adolescent, I had prayed thousands of times for God to send his guardian angels to watch over me, and had been told how, and had no reason to disbelieve, that once I reached heaven, my own personal angel and I would share more than a few laughs about the many occasions that it had intervened on my behalf. Hadn't God sent his angels to shut the mouths of the lions when Daniel had been lowered into their den? So too would they protect those who prayed for divine intervention—at least until, right before the Second Coming, God withdrew His presence from the earth, and the time of trouble began.

I'd never been crazy about reading about the time of trouble, never much liked the idea of having to flee into the mountains. Anyway, weren't we already there? Well, yes and no. The authorities would know where we lived. And as law-breaking Sabbath-keepers, we would need to be hunted down and brought to justice. Which meant we'd have to leave our houses behind, taking only the clothes we were wearing and, presumably, as much food as we could carry. Although my parents took me each week to a church where preachers often reminded us of the imminent time of tribulation, I have no memory of them ever talking about it in any detail at home; other than blessings before meals and prayers before bed, the particulars of our religious life were rarely openly discussed. We certainly hadn't planned for the time of trouble, hadn't built a secret bunker or, like another retired doctor we knew, stocked our basement with giant barrels of lentils and rice. I'd always imagined us crawling through dense woods on our knees, limbs plastered with wet leaves, seeking shelter in damp caves. There, we'd sing hymns. Recite memory verses. Watch beams of light from roving helicopters as they cast crazed shadows upon forest floors. Unleash impassioned prayers for protection. And await that cloud of angels we'd know would soon appear in the sky to take us home.

I have to believe that my grandmother, by suggesting I read about the time of trouble, had no intention of tormenting me. My guess was that she recognized my sour attitude as an inherent weakness—a spiritual frailty of sorts—and therefore worried that if I couldn't handle the small disappointments of everyday existence, I couldn't be expected to fare very well during the time of the end, when I'd be forced to hide from would-be persecutors in a cave with only the promises of the word of God—which I had been implored to collect in the storehouse of my memory—to keep me warm.

I'd never been a fan of Ellen G. White. Never fully trusted her. In photographs, she appeared in her shapeless, prim black dresses. That she could not, under any circumstances, be said to have an attractive appearance, save for the illustrations that depicted her as a young woman while bathed in a kind of heavenly light during one of her many visions—was often discussed as if it were some sort of positive character trait, a kind of humility that had the effect of ennobling her. But it wasn't her appearance that bothered me. It was her words.

"Have you read *Steps to Christ?*" someone—a friend, a relative—would say. I had not. My slim, leatherbound copy of this book—emblazoned with my name on the cover in gold—sat untouched in a gilded cardboard box.

One could assert—as Sister White might've—that I had sins I was relishing, and that in my psychologically disfigured state my heart had become hardened. That is, the fact that I didn't like to read the work of Ellen White revealed that there was something wrong with me. She was God's messenger, a person whose writing had been inspired by the same Holy Spirit that had led the writers of scripture. To reject her, then, was to reject the Holy Spirit's message. And to reject God.

On March 27, 2020, the president of the university where I'd been teaching for nearly fifteen years sent a message to students, faculty, and staff.

In recent days, he wrote, *the first confirmed cases of Novel Coronavirus (COVID-19) in Southwest Virginia have emerged.*

Included among these cases is a member of the Virginia Tech community, a student living off campus in Blacksburg who is believed to have been exposed during recent international travel. According to the New River Health District, our student is receiving care and has been in self-isolation, with no known exposures to the public. There is no evidence of a risk of community spread and we wish the student a quick recovery.

A friend on Twitter asked if the student had contracted the virus in a vacuum and flown an empty plane home.

"Shoutout to the solitary teleporter," I tweeted.

In New York, deaths from the virus had jumped to 2,000.

The Columbia Sportswear CEO cut his own salary to $10,000 a year, so that he could keep paying employees.

More than one person was talking about how these days everybody's life resembled an Edward Hopper painting.

Big Evan texted to say that the night before, he'd seen a handful of bonfires in the neighborhood of student rental houses where he lived.

But these kids, they hadn't been partying.

They'd been staring somberly—and soberly—into the flames.

A Black man named George Floyd was killed by a policeman who, after detaining him, knelt on his throat for over eight minutes. A video of Floyd's final moments, as he used his last breath to call out for his mother, went viral. Now, people were protesting in cities all over America, all over the world. Even in Blacksburg. I watched hours of video from these protests on TikTok; it was literally the only thing I could think of to do. A Black man removed a skateboard from the hands of a young white man who appeared to be attempting to use it to bash in the window of a barbershop. Thousands of people walked along a highway in the middle of a city I couldn't identify. Thousands more lay down on an eight-lane stretch. People in masks looted stores. A woman pretended to use some kind of floppy and obviously ineffective material to beat against a window, perhaps as a way to mock looters. A giant white man threatened members of a group who were chanting "peaceful protest." An English performer named Jon Hopkins, who, according to his website, felt "paralyzed by this situation," posted a recording he'd completed of himself playing a 100-year-old singing bowl that he'd purchased in a shop in India. A man walked past a toothless and possibly insane old woman lying in a city flowerbed, and said to her, "Hello, you beautiful vegetable." I didn't know what to do, either. So I kept swiping and tapping my screen, as if, however improbably, I might land on something that might explain the chaos into which the world, despite its blooming, was descending. As if such a thing—an explanation—was the cure for our collective illnesses.

Twenty-four years before—during the spring of my senior year of college at the University of North Carolina at Chapel Hill—I'd met a young stranger who wanted to know if I wanted to talk about the bible. He wore a beard and ponytail, an oversized parka (holes in the polyester exposing white fluff beneath), but several layers of shirts, and what looked like at least two pairs of pants. He appeared to be reading a pocket-sized New Testament.

I did not want to talk about the Bible. I didn't want to be approached by strangers. Didn't want to be converted. I wanted to be left alone. Even so, maybe because as a kid on my church's annual Ingathering Day, I had spent hours trolling parking lots and knocking on doors asking people to donate to our denomination's disaster relief program, and knew the discomfort of approaching strangers, I said, "Sure."

"Have you given your life to Christ?" New Testament boy asked.

"Yes."

"So, you're a believer?"

"Once upon a time."

"Why'd you stop?"

"I don't know. I guess I was sick of force-fed religion."

"Wait," he replied. "Could we say a prayer right here?"

I shrugged.

The guy stood up, set a grubby hand upon my shoulder, closed his eyes, and frowned earnestly as he prayed. "Father, we are so unworthy of your love. Our righteousness, as Paul said, is as filthy rags. And yet we know that you love us. You will never forget us. I ask that you now please bless this man. Only you know the secrets of his heart, his pain, his needs, his loves. I ask that he can know your love and presence in his life. In Christ, who strengthens us, Amen."

I shut my eyes quickly, then opened them. My shoulder tingled. Although I would've been reluctant to admit it, I felt a little better. Lighter. Unburdened, perhaps, after having been blessed by a fellow deadbeat.

"Thanks," I said. "Hey, can I ask you another question?"

"Sure."

"So... like, what do you do with Revelation?"

"What I *do* with it?"

"How do you interpret it?"

The guy shrugged. "Revelation's some intense stuff, man. I'm just a babe in Christ. And you don't give a baby a piece of steak to eat, right? He has to grow up, grow teeth, know how to eat the hard stuff."

Babe in Christ, I thought. Know how to eat the hard stuff. It wasn't the answer I'd expected. But I'd never forget it. This kid, who seemed as authentic as anyone I'd ever met, had shown me that it was okay to accept that there were some things you could say you didn't know. I'd had no clue a true believer would ever be allowed to accept such a thing. But the idea of not knowing, in that moment, made so much sense, so suddenly, it seemed irrefutable. Absurd, even, to imagine that we humans could ever really know anything for sure.

One night, Kelly asked me what it was gonna be like after the pandemic was over. I told her that if worse came to worst, we could retreat to my dad's house and start a commune. And if things got really bad, we could just fix ourselves vodka-cyanide cocktails.

I'd been thinking about the Heaven's Gate cult. It had been twenty-three years since the day when the cult's thirty-nine members, all of whom were dressed in identical costumes—black pants and black Nikes with white swooshes—had chased a concoction of phenobarbital and applesauce with vodka, placed plastic bags around their heads, and died. On their last night on earth, they'd all visited a Marie Callendar's restaurant, to enjoy a last supper. According to the *L. A. Times*, one of the waiters said that they'd all ordered the same thing. That everything had been set up before they arrived.

"They all had iced teas to drink," the waiter said. "Dinner salads beforehand with tomato vinegar dressing. Turkey pot pie for the entree. Cheesecake with blueberries on top for dessert. They seemed very nice, very friendly, very polite. No one seemed depressed at all, or anything like that."

And perhaps they hadn't been. Just as I could understand the allure of absolute and total rebellion—hookers, blow, etc.—so too could I imagine the sweet relief of acquiescing one's will, of handing it over to somebody else, of agreeing to a system of beliefs in which the kind of thoughts one could think were limited to those one's leaders had approved. What to wear? Already decided. What to order? Taken care of. A life in which you were so sure of what you believed that you laid yourself down on a bed and died. Whether the members of Heaven's Gate were able, as they'd surely believed, to fly out of their "human containers" and onto a spaceship that was following the Comet Hale–Bopp, no one could say. But Nike discontinued the shoes that they wore, pairs of which could still be bought on the internet—assuming you had six grand to blow.

"I didn't know Marie Callendar's was a restaurant," Kelly said, when I relayed this story. She'd only seen the boxed meals in the frozen foods section of grocery stores.

Okay, fine. But had she heard about "skin hunger"? An article I'd read in *Wired* magazine described how a woman named Lucy—a thirty-one-year-old director—had been breaking the rules of lockdown to walk to the end of a garden to meet her best friend, Alice. "There," the article said, "with the furtiveness of a street drug deal," Lucy tightly hugged her friend. "You just get that rush of feeling better," Alice said. "Like it's all okay." And I had to suppose—because I hugged Kelly every morning when she kindly brought me coffee in bed—that, at least for a moment, it must have felt like it maybe one day it might be.

On Sunday, May 10, 2020—Mother's Day—I stood in my father's bedroom after dark and waited. I wasn't supposed to be there: lockdown hadn't yet ended. But it was the first Mother's Day we'd celebrated since mom had died, and it'd felt necessary to break quarantine rules to visit the home over which she had presided for so long, and to be able to visit her grave. I kneeled before the window I'd raised three months before, on the night when the lights had flashed so clearly and insistently. Outside, the creek roared. Stars appeared. The darkness deepened. But no lights appeared in the woods. Not on that night. Not the following night, either. I wondered whether Luisa had turned out to be right: the phenomenon of "the lights" would not last forever. My father hadn't seen a single flash in weeks. It was unclear to me what he thought of them now, except that, in his mind, they might be "seasonal." Like snow in winter. Crocuses in spring. Thunder in summer. Dead leaves in fall. I couldn't help acknowledging, though, how the lights' gradual disappearance seemed to have coincided with something else nobody could have predicted, not even my father: the appearance, on the screen of his iPad, of a woman named Jolene.

X. LOSE YOUR MOM, LOSE THE SKY

I first learned about Jolene on that same Mother's Day weekend, which also coincided with my dad's birthday, at my parents' house, with my sister and her family. I'd been looking forward to the trip: a transgression that felt warranted—perhaps because I'd imagined, like any other selfish human who had the nerve to break the rules of quarantine, that we somehow deserved it. Before we reached I-81, I'd imagined—hoped, even—that long stretches of highway would be vacant, the way they often appeared in post-apocalyptic movies. Maybe abandoned cars would appear here and there, like the ones I plundered for scrap in *Days Gone*. I'd spent so much time playing the game recently that, once on the open road, I kept catching myself eyeballing vacant buildings, and wondering whether they might be worth searching, to replenish zombie-slaughtering supplies: bandages, ammo, and kerosene, rags, and beer bottles for Molotov cocktails. But the interstate, as it turned out, was packed. Tractor trailers, trucks, cars, vans, RVs, the works. Digital signs above the road announced government mandates to STAY HOME. But here we all were, on the highway, the majority of us exceeding the speed limit by fifteen miles per hour. There weren't enough cops in existence to pull us over. Maybe they no longer cared.

We arrived at Dad's at midday. The gravel road that wound up the mountain to his place had been gutted by storms, forty-five inches of precipitation so far for 2020. A record. Creeks gushed. The woods were alive with flowers, bees, and new green leaves. It was as if whatever had made COVID so powerful had also nourished the wilderness. Inside the house, I found myself staring at paintings my mother had made of bouquets. Distant mountains. Seaside windmills. A portrait, taken by a professional photographer, of my mother at sixteen. My mother at twenty-one in her bridal gown.

"Say hello to Jolene," my father said. He pointed his iPad at me.

"Hello," I said.

"Hello," Jolene replied. Thanks to the poorly lit video, I couldn't see her face that well. Didn't think much of it. Even when I learned that my father and Jolene had been talking for weeks, via Facetime, for hours at a time, I shrugged. After all, she was a friend of the family. Or had been, once upon a time. She'd been an old college classmate of Dad's. She'd recently separated from her husband. And had worked as a dental hygienist for fifty years. In Guam. Half a world away. fourteen hours ahead.

Jolene lived in the future.

"It's purely for companionship," my father claimed, to explain why he'd been talking to Jolene so often—and for so long. My sister was skeptical. I asked why. After all, hadn't a seventy-three-year-old man—one who'd spent the previous ten years taking care of our mother as she slipped slowly away—earned the right to do whatever he wanted? She supposed he had. But that didn't mean she had to like it. Also, she wasn't crazy about the way he'd been character-izing the relationship. A man and woman, in her opinion, simply could not talk for hours a day for weeks on end and not develop feelings for one another. I wondered. My father, who'd bought, because of our shared love of them, a pack of Hebrew National hot dogs, shoved two on a double-pronged metal stick and thrust them into his brand-new wood stove, where orange coals crackled. Once they'd been satisfactorily blistered, he lifted them out and up to me. For some reason, this made me think of the ending of Leonard Michael's story, "My Father," where the narrator, going out for the night, meets his father coming home from his barber shop. The father tells the son he needs a haircut. That he looks like a bum. Then he gives him a few coins for the subway.

"He gave," Leonard wrote, in the story's final lines. "I took."

Would Jolene from Guam someday come for a visit? Would things between her and my dad get serious? I wasn't sure I wanted to know. It seemed unlikely. But also? Quite possible. Then again, what could "serious" even look like for two septuagenarians? Having returned to Virginia, I'd been continuing to keep, if halfheartedly, a quarantine diary, which acted as a kind of release valve for the pressures of the pandemic, but I'd also been squandering far too many hours playing *Days Gone*. Disappointingly, I'd decimated all the zombie hordes. I texted my friend Ron, who'd also finished the game.

You saved the world, Ron said. *But not yourself.*

No more zombies. The fun was over. Yes, I had won. But also? I'd lost.

I opened Google Earth and typed "Guam" into the search box. The globe spun. The screen zoomed into the south Pacific to an island in what looked to me like the middle of nowhere. I dragged the little yellow stick figure onto a random road and was transported to a generic-looking landscape. Nondescript houses. Trucks. A two-lane road bisected by a single line. Tropical plants. Convenience stores with banners advertising Bud Light. Elsewhere on the island, the U.S. Naval base, and miles and miles of white sand beaches and clear blue water, high-end resorts surrounded by palm trees.

This is what Jolene was leaving behind.

To come to rural North Carolina.

To my dad.

Two weeks after we visited my father on Mother's Day weekend, he drove to Blacksburg to visit. Not long after he arrived, we went for a walk together. He informed me that he'd just re-opened his dental office. And that one of his assistants had been upset with him; she'd wanted to know whether it'd be okay if she kept collecting unemployment—which was more than she'd been making as a regular employee—and then "volunteer" at my father's office.

"Only if you want to commit fraud," my father had said.

As it turned out, my dad had some strange ideas about Covid. "I worked as a dentist for forty-five years without ever wearing a mask," he told me. He wasn't fond of the idea. Something about discomfort. Something else about the supposed harmfulness of breathing one's own CO_2, despite the fact that medical professionals the world over had been wearing them as a precautionary measure for decades. Something else about supposedly lowered oxygen levels he predicted mask wearers would experience. Furthermore, in all of his mask-less years, he'd been sick maybe two or three times. Decades of close proximity to his patients and their various ailments, he presumed, had bolstered his immune system. Oh, and his mother had been struck with influenza when he'd been a fetus in her womb. That might be, he'd surmised, why he'd never contracted any variety of influenza. He knew Covid was different. But come on! It was making us all crazy!

I wanted to ask my father if he ever thought that he might be predisposed to believing conspiracy theories, especially because the denomination to which he belonged promoted the idea that Satan was conspiring against God to hoodwink humanity out of salvation. But I kept my mouth shut.

"If we're all eventually going to get it," he said, "we oughta all go ahead and just get it."

Even though I'd had the same stupid thought, I took a second to admonish him, if only in the privacy of my head.

Old girlfriends, he said, had been texting him. Women with names like "Mariellen" and "Candy," the latter of whom had once bailed him out of jail after teenage dad had gotten pulled for a speeding ticket and couldn't pay the ticket, and had subsequently invited him to her house, where he'd stayed overnight on a bed in the basement, and where Candy, dressed in a revealing negligee, had spent a long time talking to him. He'd wanted to bust a move but, fearing rejection perhaps, he hadn't been able to get up the nerve. Meanwhile, in the present day, a seventy-some-year-old patient had asked him recently, whether or not anybody had been bringing him casseroles. My father's staff assured him that she'd been flirting.

"Guess you're back in the game," I mumbled.

He laughed.

"What about the lights?" I asked, in an attempt to change the subject to one I cared more about.

"What about them?"

"Seen any recently?"

"No," he said. "Not for weeks. Probably not since I started talking to Jolene."

In my mind, I often replayed what Luisa said about the lights:

I felt your mother's presence and energy...

She'd had a profound spiritual experience during the last ten years of her life...

She got eighty-two lifetimes of learning and experience and expanding beyond her own conditioning...

Your mom was one of these people who's a kind of light beam generator...

She found the light...

She desperately wants your dad to know that life is so much bigger...

Sandra is so grateful that you've noticed and that you're looking deeper. But actually? This is more for your dad...

She would like to move on to the "Big Light"...

These lights...will not continue indefinitely...

I would hope for her sake...they would not...

I found myself in a strange position: wanting to see that benevolent flash in the distance, and also hoping I never would. I hadn't talked to my dad about the lights much, except to inquire as to whether he'd seen any. His answer? Not much at all. It would have been nice to tell him about my session with Luisa, to explain how she'd said that the lights had been for him, but it didn't make sense to bother him with all that. I knew that if I were to tell him anything about her, he'd only worry about me.

Jolene and Dad could talk—and did talk—for hours on end.

"I can tell her anything," Dad said. "I can even talk about your mom with her. And she's fine with that. She knew her. She respected her." This talking, my father said, was the most gratifying thing about their friendship. For years, my father claimed, he'd been envious of Kelly and me, and of my sister and her husband. We could all hold deep conversations with one another. He'd never really been able to have those kinds of talks with my mother.

I knew what he meant. My mother had always been very good at giving the impression that she was listening. But it had always been difficult to gauge how closely. "Uh huh," she'd say. And "That's right!" And "If that isn't the limit!" I don't think it mattered if she agreed or not. I have vague memories of eavesdropping on conversations, and hearing people say things that I knew for a fact she didn't believe or wouldn't endorse, but—perhaps to keep the conversation going—she'd contributed a series of affirmations. I used to joke to people that I could call my mother and when she asked about my day I could say "well today I got up and made my son's lunch" and she'd say "Uh-huh" and then I'd say, "and then I walked the dog" and she'd say, "Uh-huh" and then I'd say, "and then I stabbed my wife to death and put her body in a freezer" and she'd say "Uh-huh" again. I was exaggerating, obviously. But it wasn't far from how I perceived our interactions.

Now, Dad had found a receptacle for his stories—but

more importantly, perhaps, he'd finally become a receptacle for someone else's. Had he ever confided to my mother—as he had once to me—that, for twenty years, he'd fantasized about a button he could press that would erase him from the world without hurting anyone else? I doubted it. He wouldn't have wanted to burden her with that knowledge. And my mother, I don't think, ever confided in him, at least not about her own fears and anxieties. Whatever she might have had to confess she buried so deep I doubt that even she would have known how to find it.

Later that night, my father announced that he was going out to his Highlander, to FaceTime Jolene; he didn't want to talk in the guest bedroom and disturb Kelly, who'd already turned in. He was carrying his iPad. He asked if I wanted to join. I said no. I did not want to talk to Jolene. Talking to Jolene—on Facetime, no less—would make her more real. And I did not want Jolene to be real. Not now. Not yet.

Ten minutes later, my curiosity got the best of me. And I was like *fuck it*.

I went outside.

I liked to think that, during our first conversation, Jolene and I had hit it off. Charming, inquisitive, unassuming, chirpy, attractive, and quick-witted, she reminded me of a seventy-three-year-old Kristen Wiig, the actor on *Saturday Night Live* known for her characters "Target Lady" and "Penelope."

Jolene and I talked about books; she was a big reader, loved historical fiction. I asked her if she knew that my father didn't much like to read. Dad tried to act like he did and I was like, "Yeah the Bible and the internet. Nothing else." Jolene thought this was very interesting; she hadn't known this about my father.

"She's really into music," Dad said.

"Oh!" Jolene exclaimed. "I love music!"

"What do you like?"

"A little bit of everything," she said. "I listened to the Beach Boys today. And Aretha Franklin."

"Dad only likes Merle Haggard."

"Oh really?"

"I do like him a lot," my dad said.

Jolene looked up Merle Haggard on another device. Once she found concert footage, she turned the screen so we could see it.

Jolene, I was learning, was easy to talk to.

The next morning, Dad and I went for another walk. Dad said that this thing with Jolene seemed like pretty much a done deal, did it not? And said that it was nice to have my blessing. I reminded him I'd never actually said that. As we walked, I texted my sister, to tell her about talking to Jolene. Said it was "pretty fun."

Carrie said, "Don't say that" and "I'm not ready to like her yet." But she wanted more details. So, I called and put her on speaker phone. But she didn't want to be on speaker phone because then we couldn't talk behind Dad's back. I put her on speakerphone anyway. And then I told her that Jolene was a good conversationalist. That she had a good sense of humor. That she liked the Beatles and the Beach Boys and Aretha Franklin. And that she was a big reader. My sister wasn't having it. Dad said that Jolene might be going with Uncle Ted and Aunt Nancy and him to Lake Sunapee during their annual trip to New Hampshire. Carrie *really* didn't seem to like this. Dad said that Ted and Nancy could be their chaperones. Carrie wondered if they were planning to sleep in the same bed.

"Yes," Dad said, "but with a rolled-up quilt between us."

I said, "If all goes well, maybe Uncle Ted could marry them right there. But then," I added, knowing this was the last thing either of them would ever want, "they wouldn't get to have a big wedding. Like down by the pond at Dad's house. Or better yet, beside mom's grave."

My sister replied by saying, "She has to fit into Mom's wedding dress. If she can't, they're not allowed to get married." My sister wanted to know what kind of grand-mother Jolene had been. Had she made homemade cards for her grandchildren?

Dad assured us that there was no way Jolene could ever replace our mother.

"She'll just be sleeping in the bed where Mom died," I added.

"No," my sister said. "If that happened Dad would have to switch sides," meaning he'd had to sleep on the left side rather than the right. Dad said that yesterday that he'd told Jolene that I'd said that I'd always wanted a brother. Jolene had said she wasn't sure that her son and I would get along. Dad said her son was covered in tattoos. My sister wanted to know what that had to do with anything. Dad didn't know. But when we reached the top of the golf course, the flag that flew on a pole between the clubhouse and garage was at half-mast.

A grad student named Kira, who'd served as my teaching assistant the previous fall, messaged to ask whether I knew if Virginia Tech planned to reopen for classes next semester. I said I didn't know. That, in my opinion, nobody did. I did know that the university had already decided that anyone who elected to teach online in the fall could do so, and that classes that were meeting in actual physical spaces would do so according to the rules of social distancing, which meant that a classroom with forty-eight seats would allow for only a class of twelve, and that students and teachers would be required to wear masks, and that students who refused to wear masks would be escorted out of buildings by persons whose job it would be to enforce these rules, about which I first learned last week at a departmental meeting. During this meeting, I had scrolled through the photos of my colleagues, like so many participants in the 1970s game show *Hollywood Squares*. Many of the meeting's participants had elected not to enable video, so only their selected profile photo or simply their names, in white letters against an ominous black background, appeared. One of my friends had taken to playing Departmental Bingo with his wife and Kelly and me, a game which involved making predictions concerning what our colleagues would likely say or do during these meetings, like whether or not so-and-so would sigh heavily or whether Big Evan would begin a question directed at our chair with the phrase, "Could it be the case..." or whether a particular attendee would attempt to argue that instructors were the so-called backbone of our department. My Department Bingo friend had noted that one of our instructors, whose image was backlit and thus illegible against the brightness of a window she was sitting in front of, looked as if she were "an anonymous whistleblower on a 60 *Minutes* report," while I noted that another of our professors looked as if she was participating in a virtual séance circa 1844. At any rate, it was during this meeting, when my colleagues were typing up question after question that could not be answered—"how would the town of Blacksburg prevent students from holding large gatherings?" and "do we know if extracurricular events will be held on or around campus?" and "what will the bars be doing so that students don't congregate there?"—that I decided that, as much as I hated to do this, that I would, rather than stare out at a classroom of masked students while trying to project my own voice through a mask I would have to wear (I think now about that black and white Joy Division *Unknown Pleasures* mask that was sitting unpurchased in my Red Bubble shopping cart) as I taught, hold my classes online, via Zoom. I told this to Kira and she—anticipating that once the students returned, the virus would "spread like wildfire" and she would rather not be forced to "be around a bunch of dumbass eighteen-year-olds"—agreed.

Kira told me about her friend whose dad caught it. I had sent a message announcing that I had lost everything I'd written in the last week, a confession that now seemed almost trivial with the prospect of a young person losing both her parents in a global pandemic, and so when she asked me how I'd lost all that work, I'd felt sheepish and said, *Well it hardly matters in the face of losing a life* and *also IDK!*

While I also explained to her that the writing I'd been working on had to do with Dad and Jolene, a recap that prompted Kira to send me the "mind blown" emoji with the surprised face and what looked like an atomic explosion blasting the top of the round face's head off, I did not tell her that the thought of having to say, for as long as they remained together, supposing they even got together for real, the phrase "Dad and Jolene" filled me with a chest-tightening load of dread.

There's a Vietnamese proverb, I added, *that I'll probably butcher now but it's something like, if you lose your dad, it's like the roof blew off your house, but if you lose your mom, you lose... the SKY.*

And that's when we turned our attention to the fact that nostalgic teens had been making TikTok videos of past teenagers from the 2010s, commenting on how much happier and more alive they appeared. Everything seemed, as it had for weeks, so impossibly far away; perhaps that's why I thought then about the concept of cottagecore, I remembered that my friend Nic, a professor of creative writing and former drummer for a band who'd charted a Top 10 hit and appeared on *The Tonight Show*, had sent me a text last fall that his wife, Abby, had read on an online forum, and so I scrolled through six months of conversations to find what he'd sent: Would it be possible to revive the old tradition of Sister Circles? This is what I remember from the 1990s. All the sisters gather at a lovely homestead. Everyone is dankly dressed in patchwork and scented with oils. Mamas are baking bread, which the loaves get wrapped in dish towels. Then we hug them, sing a heartsong and give each other the loaves which we break off and feed to each other hot and fresh. We brush each other's hair and bathe each other's feet in big bowls of cornmeal with lavender flowers in it. Meanwhile kids and dogs are running around playing happily. In the middle of the floor is a massive pile of every gorgeous hippie thing you can think of. Sisters are welcome to take anything they want. We'd sing our thank yous and turn each others names into songs. The men chopped wood outside and built a nice bonfire. Later we would sit around the bonfire and pass big jars of mushroom honey tea and drum and sing heartsongs as the kids fell asleep on blankets on our laps. I would definitely make huge efforts to be part of a sister swap like that. The previous October, I couldn't have helped but make fun of this request, but now, I was hard-pressed to think these benevolent weirdos might be onto something—and that I too might enjoy visiting, assuming such a place had ever actually existed in the world, if only to sing a heartsong or two.

Please don't write about this, my sister instructed me, via text message. It was day Day 59 of quarantine in Virginia, Day 57 for those living in Tennessee. The death toll was about to reach 100,000. On Twitter, the President had promoted a conspiracy theory supporting the idea that former congressman and TV pundit Joe Scarborough was responsible for the death of Lori Klaustis, a woman who once worked for Scarborough. But Carrie wasn't talking about that. She'd recently spoken with our father, who'd told her the story he'd told me about Jolene. The one I wasn't supposed to share—and hadn't.

The story went something like this: once upon a time, Jolene had lived in Lincoln, Nebraska. For a short time— one academic year—my father had also lived in Lincoln, where he'd attended, along with Jolene and her boyfriend Dick, Union College, a Seventh-day Adventist institution. Apparently, my dad had spent a lot of time hanging out with

Jolene and Dick. I didn't know what, exactly, the three of them did together, but I do know that this was the one year that my father had really let loose, the year he'd smoked his first cigarette and drank his beer and drank enough Southern Comfort one night to swear off the stuff forever. Fast forward fifty-some years. Jolene and Dick were now separated, with plans to divorce. During one of her conversations with my father, Jolene had reminded him about the time back in Nebraska that he'd approached her with an odd proposal: If she left Dick, he'd leave his fiancée, my future mother, and they—my father and Jolene, that is—could be together. There very well may be an alternate universe where these things unfolded, and where my mother and father, instead of marrying and having my sister and me, instead went their separate ways. But in this one, they didn't. Jolene refused my father's advances.

"I could never do that to Sandra," is what she'd told him, despite the fact that she had yet to meet her. I don't know if Mom ever knew about this but, thanks to her refusal, my sister and I exist.

Now my face looks like shit, Carrie texted. She was pulling a twelve-hour shift at East Tennessee Medical Group, where, for the last several months, she'd been tasked with testing patients for COVID-19.

Why does your face look like shit? I replied.

Cause I've been crying, she said, *and once I start, I really start.*

I texted my sister a sad face I made by typing a colon and a left-facing parenthesis, and asked her what she was thinking.

Just how screwed up it seems, she said. *Like now that mom's dead, dad can be with the girl he wanted.*

Yeah, but it's not like Dad had spent all these years pining.

I know, my sister replied. *But he's said they communicate so well, better than he and mom ever did. It hurts to hear that. Not like I thought they had the perfect marriage. But like now he can really be fulfilled. I know I probably seem juvenile. Like I'm jealous on behalf of mom.*

Listen. Mom's ten-year decline and death was super messed up. Everything after would have to be a shitshow of sorts. I personally would rather dad be single so I could go home and be in his house which is like a freaking tomb mom built herself for us to grieve her absence. But that's not fair to him. Or to Jolene.

I actually found myself daydreaming about being good friends with Jolene and wondering if that will happen, my sister texted. *I really hope it does. Dad asked if I wish I hadn't told him. I felt bad for crying. I don't want him to feel bad.*

Our lives, I assured her, *are built upon the stories we tell about them and when we realize that something is more complicated, we freak out.*

I think my brain is broken, my sister replied.

All brains are broken. We like to believe in the things we told ourselves about our families, because, in doing so, we could take chaos and give it, as so many of us preferred, especially in times that so many people were now calling uncertain, the appearance of order.

Mimi called to wish me a happy birthday. Said she hoped I had wonderful dreams in which my mother had returned from the dead. In fact, Mimi said that she'd dreamed, the night before, that she'd spent the day shopping with her own mother, in Paris. I told her that I'd dreamed that a woman named Kristen, who serves as the bookkeeper for Virginia

Tech's English department and had decorated her office with *Star Wars* memorabilia, tested me for Covid. I was positive.

On the weekend of July the 4th, we drove down to my father's house to visit again. It was hot. The streams were as high as I'd ever seen them. Elijah's friend, Oscar, who accompanied us, used a wet rock to paint abs on his stomach. We swam in the pond. Dad did a backflip off the dock. We got takeout from Burger Basket, home of the world's finest cheeseburgers, where I overheard somebody float an idea about a possible Civil War and another somebody joke-order the "Hunter Biden Special," to which the woman behind the counter said that if she served that she'd be afraid of poisoning someone. We watched the quarter-of-a-century-old video of my dad tormenting my grandmother by trying to show her a rattlesnake he'd caught and dumped out on the driveway. We visited Mom's grave—a mound of earth that had been outlined in stones from the creek and topped with a patchwork of moss and ferns. And after sundown, we stared into the dark, hoping for the telltale flashes.

We didn't see anything.

What we didn't know: the weekend before we'd arrived, one of the hygienists that worked for my father had gone—despite the ban on gatherings of more than ten people—to her son's wedding that'd included an attendee who'd been known to have contracted the virus. Dad had sent the hygienist home the day before we arrived. She'd felt sick. Had been coughing. Soon the entire office had it, including my father, who, though we'd spent an entire weekend with us, hadn't bothered to tell us that he'd been exposed—until after we'd left.

Back in Virginia, we paid a visit to our nearest testing center. The woman who greeted us wore what looked like a pretend astronaut suit made of paper and transparent plastic. A ribbed tube snaked from the back of her head. She stuck a tiny wand into our nostrils. But first she took our temperatures. Mine was lower than normal. Kelly's was higher. Elijah had a legit fever at 100-point something.

Even so, two days later, our tests came back negative. Kelly was relieved. Elijah had no visible reaction. But I couldn't help but be disappointed. I'd aspired to be asymptomatic. But that would've only fixed me. Had I contracted the virus and survived, I would've gained immunity. But the rest of the world would still be on fire.

Dad claimed he'd never got that sick. Eventually, he recovered. But he wouldn't be going to Guam, like he'd planned. Jolene would come here, to the States. They'd be married at the Justice of the Peace after Dad picked her up from the Atlanta airport.

No way, I thought. *They're moving too fast.*

Had my dad's sister heard this news? She had. And his brother? Yep. I'd called both of them on the phone. Expressed my concerns. They shared their own. And agreed I should call their brother.

"I don't want you to do something that your younger self would be embarrassed by or that your future self would regret," I told my father, over the phone. "It's like you boarded a train going a thousand miles an hour. You're gonna crash into the station if you don't slow down."

"What else should I do? It's not like we have many years left."

"I'm not against you getting married. I just think you should wait an appropriate amount of time. I don't want to meet Jolene for the first time as your wife."

"What *would* be an appropriate amount of time?"

"I don't know. I only know what an inappropriate amount of time looks like."

Time, as expected, passed. Scientists discovered that humans consuming their own fecal microbiomes might help dieters who wanted to lose weight and that the earth was once home to "terror crocodiles" the size of city buses. The owners of a Michigan funeral home realized that a woman who'd been dead was actually alive. The bubonic plague showed up in China's Inner Mongolia. Perfume designers constructed a cologne that smelled like "outer space." Kelly looked out the window and said it looked hazy and I said that it was summer and she said, "No, it's not that" and when she learned about the Saharan dust cloud felt vindicated. The president's men tear gassed protestors in front of a church so he could pose with an upside-down bible. Monkeys stole vials of coronavirus blood samples from lab workers. A woman who illegally entered Yellowstone fell into a thermal feature while taking pictures. Japanese honeybees learned how to "cook" a murder hornet. Inmates were caught on video trying to infect themselves with coronavirus. After a decade-long search, a man found a treasure worth more than one million dollars in the Rocky Mountains. My sister began texting Jolene. My father asked why I hadn't been. I told him it was because I didn't want to. And a woman's last words before being eaten by an alligator were, "Well, I guess I won't do this again."

On July 31st, I returned to my father's house to help sort out the possessions my mother had left behind. To clear space, as it were, for Jolene. I rolled into town and stopped at my father's office. His employees weren't sure what to think about "the Jolene situation." Sharon, the woman who worked the front desk, said that she'd suggested that Dad purchase new socks, T-shirts, and underwear.

"You don't want to go around with holey drawers," she added.

Would any of them want their husbands to remarry? Michell said nobody else on earth could put up with her husband. Sharon said she wouldn't want hers to. Tamara said she wished her ex would find somebody. Kelly never answered.

"She don't even know what he smells like," Tamara said.

"He told Jolene that," I said. "And she said, 'Wait. You smell?'"

"That's funny, actually."

"I miss your mom coming in," Sharon said. "She was always so happy."

"Can you believe that it was only two years ago that she and dad went to Switzerland to hike the Alps?" I said. At the time, there had been some concern about taking that last trip. Not that she didn't have the physical wherewithal to embark on thirteen-mile hikes. According to Carrie, despite the fact that our mom would get confused in the chalet, forget which bathroom was hers, and needed help getting dressed, she'd plodded along during those hikes, *oohing* and *ahh*ing as she always had, over the beauty of alpine flora and fauna.

"I bet our parking lot hasn't been swept once since she died," Michell said, referencing the relatively short period of time when, unable to leave her for long stretches, dad would bring her to the office, where she'd find simple little chores to pass the time.

"She was always getting up on the bank behind the office."

"To weed?"

"Yes. And we'd tell her to come down. We didn't want her to fall. And she'd just throw her head back and roar with laughter."

I smiled.

"It's just a lot," Michell said.

"2020 has been wild," I added.

"You can say that again."

Dad told me that he and Carrie and her husband had recently visited the family cemetery. The question arose concerning where dad and Jolene would be buried. He said that he'd be buried to the left of mom and that Jolene would be buried on his left. On Resurrection morning, my mom would be in for a surprise.

"Yeah," I said. "She'll wonder why you weren't raised up."

He laughed.

I was joking but I wasn't. Part of me wanted very badly for my father to have to suffer. I knew that he already had. But I couldn't help it. I didn't want him to be alone but I also didn't want him to marry someone who was a stranger to me. It was selfish of me to wish for him to spend the rest of his days by himself, missing mom. It seemed to my still-grieving mind like that was what she deserved.

My sister and I removed clothes from hangers, marveling at how much our mother had owned. How many outfits that we never remembered her wearing. So many shoes. She'd always believed in looking nice. Especially for church.

We emptied the closet. At some point, I mentioned how fucked up it all seemed. Carrie agreed. I retrieved a strip of toilet paper to dab my eyes. I couldn't say it was unfair. Too many human beings had suffered fates worse than mine: to be raised by a mother who loved you to death and smothered you with affection, and then died decades before anyone who knew her would have expected. We checked pockets, found breath mints and ChapStick and crinkled receipts from before either of us had been born. Filled a dozen black heavy duty garbage bags, threw them into the back of my car. Drove to a thrift store. Carried the bags through light rain to a donation shed, tossed them unceremoniously inside.

"I feel like we just abandoned her there," my sister said.

"Well," I replied. "In a way we did."

"It's like she just died all over again."

"Like she does every day."

In the middle of the last night at Dad's house, I awoke to darkness, stumbled to the bathroom, sat down on the toilet, and peed. Then shuffled back to bed. Before I lay back down, I looked out the window. I tapped the tip of my dead finger against the glass. I squinted. Waited. Whispered, "Mom." The creek, thanks to more recent rain, was gushing. No light appeared. Not even in the sky. I hoped for something. A flash. A blink. Even the ray of light from the local airport down in the valley, the one that you could see at night swooping every few seconds across the heavens. But only darkness greeted me, so I returned to bed and fell into troubled dreams.

As we continued to clean, I set aside souvenirs. I took all the pens my father had received in the past twenty years as gifts: rectangular boxes that flipped open to reveal silver wands in beds of satin. The key to my parents' honeymoon room at the Hyatt Regency, attached by a ring to a heavy metal square embossed with the image of the iconic blue spaceship-like dome that, according to my father, had once been the tallest building in Atlanta, but now was dwarfed by three-times-as-high skyscrapers. A tiny glass container with a rounded silver lid, inside of which lay the necklace my father had given my mother when she'd agreed to go steady with him in 1962, upon which hung a smooth, coinlike disc engraved with the word "Lummox," which, I learned, meant "clumsy, stupid person" but had once been used by couples as a term of endearment. Another glass container filled with coins, some of which I presumed to be pure silver. A photo of my mother wearing a floral print dress with a giant square lace collar around her neck, smiling prettily: a rare photograph in which she was the sole subject.

Near the end of *2500 Random Things about Me Too*, the author, a visual artist named Matias Viegener, said, "I no longer delete people from my address book when they die. I haven't done it in years. It feels like I am killing them." I realized that I felt like this, too. How many times had I scrolled past my father-in-law's name and thought "he's been dead for X many years now"? Too many to count. But there was his name: "Phil." Funny that his name came to my mind when I read that passage and not my own mother's. Huh, I thought. I wondered what would happen if I tried to call her. My first thought, however stupid, was that she would answer. I could hear her bright "Hello?" in my head. But what if she really did answer? What if, by some inter-dimensional miracle, I could have a conversation with her? I didn't believe that could happen. Even so, I picked up my phone. I tapped the green circle with the white phone icon—the one, like the floppy disc save button in Word—depicted the kind of outdated mechanism nobody used anymore. I scrolled past names in my contacts until I came to "Mom." I tapped the number and waited. If nothing else, I thought, I might hear Mom's voice imploring me to leave a message. "The person you have reached is not available," a voice said. If I wished, I could leave a message for "Billy White." I quickly tapped the red circle on my screen. Mom's contact info appeared. I tapped edit. And then scrolled all the way down, to delete. And then she was gone.

On the anniversary of my mother's death, I received a text from Nancy—a woman who lived in Montana with her husband and three children but had once been one of the most beautiful girls at the Adventist boarding school I attended, so far out of reach for me that I wasn't self-conscious about trying to make her laugh in our keyboarding class.

Sending extra good juju, prayers, and a long-distance hug. I didn't know your mom passed away on 9-11. Double suck.

Thank you," I texted back. *I woke up and cried for two hours. Didn't see that coming.*

Crying like that is cathartic. I wonder if you'll feel lighter later?

I already do. There may be more to come. I've found myself flash-flooded with grief when I least expect it.

So, Jolene and your dad . . . they're going to get married?

YES, I typed.

Ahh. I was going to ask. I would love to sit down with someone who has remarried after the death of a spouse and pick apart their brain with all kinds of intrusive questions that a polite person would never ask.

She texts me good morning almost every day with a cheerful 'hope you have a stress-free day' and a photo of the sunset from the night before that one of her kids in Guam sends.

Are you okay with that?

I don't know. I sort of have to be. If only because she's made my dad so happy.

Do you think your dad has any guilt?

No. Mom and Jolene actually got to eventually know each other. I really do think Mom would have wanted this.

I think you mentioned that before.

She would've wanted him to be happy. Not lonely. Kelly says the same thing to me. That she wanted me to remarry if she dies.

Messes with a person's eschatology if you believe in an afterlife.

Isn't heaven supposed to be sexless and marriage-less?

Still. It's hard for me to wrap my head around the resurrection morning piece.

Honestly that would not be the most difficult thing for me to wrap my head around, re: "resurrection morning." Dead people coming to life. Etc.

Believing that will happen, is what's difficult for you?

Correct.

I get that, Nancy texted.

And even though I knew we didn't share the same beliefs, I felt understood.

On August 27, 2020, Jolene arrived in the states. For five days, during their brief "courting" phase, she slept in the room above my father's: my sister's old room. And then, on August 31, almost five months to the day they first Facetimed, and the day that the United States hit 6 million COVID cases, she and Dad got married at the Justice of the Peace. My father called me up afterwards, said he wanted to introduce me to "the new Mrs. Vollmer." Then he repeated the joke he'd told to the magistrate: that they'd wanted to hurry up and tie the knot "before the baby arrived."

I didn't laugh at the joke. I don't know why. Maybe it was the line about "the new Mrs. Vollmer." Dad promised that no one could replace my mother. But now he was using her name—the name she'd taken in devotion to him—to refer to someone else.

My father forwarded me pictures of Jolene's library. I'd been curious about what she read. Jacques Cousteau, *The Ocean World*. Sue Monk Kidd, *The Invention of Wings*. Leo Tolstoy, *War and Peace*. Ishmael Beah, *A Long Way Gone*. Margot Lee Shetterly, *Hidden Figures*. I texted her a message.

Hey, I just wanted to say 'nice library' but also let you know that I really am happy for you and dad. I know how rare it is to find someone who you really click with—who you can talk to, who you can be yourself with, who you can laugh with, who you can share your deepest secrets with, without being judged. I found that 21 years ago when I met my wife-to-be. I never knew, even after only a few relationships, such a thing existed, or could. I know my mom and dad had an extraordinary relationship. I bask in the fact that they had a joyful life together, especially because it resulted in the miracle of me coming out of nowhere to exist! But I'm not naive enough to think that you and he can't have an Act II and that it will be completely different and happy and full of joy and wonder. I may have been hesitant and skeptical of what you guys have found together but that's because I'm not having your experience. I was an outsider looking in and I was and still am hurting because my mom isn't here and that can't help fully feel to my self-centered heart unfair. But I have to tell you, I've enjoyed every virtual minute I've ever spent with you, you've made me laugh every time, I can see why dad has fallen in love with you, and I don't blame him one bit. If you're like K, you don't like praise or compliments or even lots of attention, but at the same time, I don't want you to think that I have any reservations about you marrying my dad. He's my favorite Boomer and the best father who ever walked the earth, even if he does have some ideas I think are questionable and simply wrong (of course he can say the same about me, which is why I love him even more, since he can overlook his mistakes in my book, even if his book needs revising LOL). I just love him so much. Anyway, I look forward to getting to know you better. I hope this isn't too much of an avalanche of emotion to send your way (you might as well get used to my earnest straightforwardness) but now that you are my father's wife, I thought it might be a good idea to send you a welcome message and know that if my dad has come to love you, then I have no choice but to love you, too, and to celebrate the new life you two will make together.

I treasure those words, Matthew, Jolene wrote back. *Thank you so much.*

XI. EYEBALLS CRYBALLS

It was nice to think it could've all been that easy. That you could cross a divide with a single text.

How do you explain what can't be explained? Moreover, how do you live with it? The story goes something like this: Mom died. Three months later, the lights appeared. Three months after that, Dad started talking to Jolene. The lights started to disappear. Three months after that, they got married. Three months after that, they had completely transformed the interior of our family home. On the one hand: Why? On the other: What did it matter? After a parent died, should you really expect anything to be the same?

I could sum it up like this: nearly a year after my mother had passed away, my father was remarried, and I was still avoiding cracks in the sidewalk.

If you happen to own a King James Bible, take a moment to flip through it. Note the sheer number of words inside. Imagine that each one of these words represents a body. As of this writing, the number of words in the King James Bible roughly corresponds to the same number of human beings who have died from Covid-19: 770,000. Worldwide, the virus has killed 5.16 million. Which means that if you wanted to use the words of bibles to represent each of the bodies that died during the pandemic, you'd need nearly seven of them. If you took one second to pronounce each word in those almost seven bibles, you'd need two months, seven days, six hours, fifty-three minutes, and twenty seconds to accomplish the feat. You might still not be able to wrap your head around that number, but I'm betting you can appreciate the magnitude. Multiply 5.16 million by ten, and you'll have the number that died of the Spanish flu. Add at least 25 million to that and you'll have the lowest estimated number of human beings who died during the bubonic plague. Add 99.75 billion and you'll have the number of people who have, since the beginning of human history, passed from this world to the next.

As difficult as it may be to believe, you will someday join that number. So will I. Some days, this prospect is terrifying: One day, not that far in the future, every person now living will have entered the great unknown. On other days, this fact is eerily comforting. The most human thing that we can do, aside from living, is to die. It's inevitable. And what point is there to fearing the inevitable? Your death won't be a problem for you. But it will be another matter for those you leave behind.

My father had, over the course of quarantine, decided to stop eating sugar. He'd lost thirty pounds. With his head freshly shaved and his new hip glasses, he looked not unlike a turtle who'd lost his shell.

Your father got a new blazer, Jolene said, in a text. *Looks sharp.*

Impossible, I replied. *Style is one thing that man doesn't have.*

She sent me a picture. My father stood in the kitchen.

He looked noticeably thinner. He was wearing a fitted coat. Button-up shirt. Pants that looked like the tag may have identified them as "skinny." The expression on Dad's face looked strange. Like he was trying not to look off guard.

Behind him, the refrigerator gleamed, silver and blank. The photos that had covered its entire surface—mostly taken by my mother, and inserted into magnetic sleeves—had been taken down.

"After a while," my father said, "you don't even see those pictures." Which, he'd claimed, was the reason he didn't mind her taking them down.

This was difficult for me to believe. As was the text I received after those photos had arrived in the mail.

I'm surprised you didn't want any of these pictures, I'd texted. *Especially the ones of you and your dad.*

I'd waited eight hours to receive his reply.

Hey cool, I said. *Appreciate you replying to me.*

I'm overwhelmed with everything, he confessed. *Wondering what to do with so many things we've collected that are meaning-ful but also thinking why would I want to keep all this stuff that I haven't looked at in 20-30 yrs. How many pictures do I need? Where do I keep them?*

Nah, it's good, I replied. *I just hope you're thinking about what you actually want and need. On my end, it's weird to get a bunch of discarded memories in the mail. I assume you can get talked into getting rid of all kinds of things. If there's something you want then make sure you say yes to that. That's all.*

To this last text, I received no reply.

I like seeing Dad happy, my sister texted me. *And then it makes me sad that he is happy. And then I feel alone in my sadness.*

You should be a writer, I replied.

Ha.

A poet.

I've never written anything good.

You just did, I assured her.

A shipping crate from Guam arrived with Jolene's things. Giant paintings of bamboo and poppies. Asian statuary that Jolene had purchased as souvenirs from her extensive travels in South Asia. Giant vases. Abstract sculptures. Stacks of books. Kitchenware. Giant lamps. Imposing bookcases with heavy glass doors. Her 2020 Lexus.

Jolene, as it turned out, preferred her stuff to my mother's. The quilt that had hung above the piano—and which one of my father's patients had made by hand—was replaced by paintings of ferns in gilded frames. The big family photo—the one my friend Todd took, just before Kelly and I married—disappeared. As did the blue plates on the walls of the kitchen. The garage became a holding cell where my mother's stuff accrued in haphazard piles.

"Mom's brain was erased over ten years," I kept telling anyone who'd listen. "And then, when she finally died, she was erased from the earth in an instant. And now, by systematically removing all the things she chose to live in that house, she's being erased from her home."

I thought of that quote from *Sum: Forty Tales of the Afterlives,* by David M. Eagleman: "There are three deaths. The first is when the body ceases to function. The second is when the body is consigned to the grave. The third is that moment, sometime in the future, when your name is spoken for the last time."

Dad claimed not to have had any idea how much value people tended to place in things. Said he was more content than he'd expected to be since Mom died. But he missed her more than ever. One night, he'd been in the bathroom, and meant to call out for Jolene. But he'd yelled Mom's name instead.

And then one day—I can't remember the reason or occasion—Jolene sent my sister a message. She'd written it to explain how much she loved my dad. How grateful she was for having found him. How, in fact, she'd never thought she could ever be so happy. But at the same time, she was haunted—that was the word she had used—by the fact that our mother's passing had served as the avenue that had led her to him. I paused. I reread the forwarded message. Jolene was 73. Had never been happier. And this after leaving behind everyone she'd ever known, just to be with Dad.

That's good, I replied.

I thought so, my sister said.

Over the next few days, the resentment I'd been feeling about the changes Jolene and Dad had been making to the house seemed to evaporate. I wasn't sure how to account for it. I wanted that house to remain a temple that my mother had created and that we could visit in order to worship her. But I also found it liberating to try to simply stop caring. It hadn't occurred to me that I could simply relinquish my resentment. I didn't have to like the changes. But also? It wasn't my house. Anything they didn't want, I was free to take. And once I realized I could, I realized that there wasn't much I really wanted. A bookcase. Some of the framed photos that had hung on the balcony hallway. An antique cabinet—one that my sister and I had been instructed, as children, never to touch. I filled it with my collection of action figures. G. I. Joes. *Star Wars* characters. Doc and Marty from *Back to the Future*. Fisher-Price Little People. Ernie and Bert. Oscar the Grouch, in his trash can: a thing that was represented, on Sesame Street, to be bigger on the inside, and thus seemed like a metaphor for so many kinds of containers, including human ones.

In the end, the resentment didn't completely disappear. Feelings, after all, aren't always easy to control. But whenever I did sense resentment rearing its head, I felt like the very least I could do was to stand back and identify it as such. It wasn't unlike how, after my mother died, the resentment of certain people that I'd been savoring—specifically the more conservative members of my extended family—more or less disappeared. I first recognized this absence on the day after my mother's memorial service. My wife and son had caught a ride back to Virginia with friends, but I'd decided to stay behind for a couple of days, with my father, his brother (a longtime and now retired Seventh-day Adventist pastor, who had achieved a certain level of worldwide fame among Adventists during the 1960s for his contributions to a Christian folk band called the Wedgwood Trio), his sister-in-law (a retired schoolteacher), my aunt (a physical therapist), and her husband (the acting president of the global Seventh-day Adventist church). At one point, in the late afternoon, we were standing around chatting in the kitchen when someone mentioned—and I can no longer remember why, except that it is a book that members of my family often mention—*The Doctor and the Damned*. This book, written by Albert Haas, a French spy during World War II, documented unimaginable horrors he suffered at the hands of Nazis in various concentration camps. Near the book's end, after the a platoon of twenty-three men from the 11th Armored Division liberated the Mauthausen concentration camp, Haas credits Major Donald Vollmer—my grandfather—for saving his life. I asked my father and relatives whether they'd ever watched *Architecture of Doom*, a documentary about how the aesthetic ideals of the Nazis, many of whom were failed artists themselves, led to the Holocaust. They had not. Might they want to? Sure. What better way to spend the afternoon after my mother died than to dial up something light on the TV?

Might I have found it somewhat ironic that I was sitting in a living room with my father and his siblings and their spouses one day after my mother's memorial service, watching a film whose main purpose seemed to be how the striving for purity and strict understandings of beauty could be understood as not only dangerous but downright apocalyptic? I did. I couldn't help how these family members of mine might think when they heard those lines in the film's opening: "The Nazi gospel warns against a world about to collapse, an eternal twilight that threatens to engulf the earth. The Nazis claim to have discovered the source of this threat and took it upon themselves to eradicate it. Purified and preserved from decay, a new Germany would arise, mightier and more beautiful than ever before." Couldn't this description of the Nazis ideological framework, energized by its apocalyptic fervor and call for purity and unity of thought, be seen to have an analogue in the Adventist belief system? I didn't mean to suggest that Adventists should be viewed as Nazis. But certain similarities between the two group's ideologies—that of the imminent apocalypse, of attempting to purify one's body so as to prepare it for inhabiting a better place, and of taking refuge in the idea of being rewarded for thinking about the world in very particular and limited ways—were making themselves known: an amplification, I was sure, that was taking place in my head because of the people who were in the room.

"Actually, you know what? They might have been on to something," my Aunt Melinda said, scrunching up her nose at the distorted figures of Cubism. She laughed—as she has always been wont to do—but then assured me she wasn't kidding. As if to say that there was definitely something not quite right about that kind of artistic expression.

At some point during the viewing of this film, I became hungry and went into the kitchen, where I opened and began to heat, over the stove, several cans of black beans. Kelly and I had been to Walmart two days before, and not knowing who or how many guests would need food or whether anyone else might bring the expected casseroles that appear in the home where someone has recently died, I decided to gather the ingredients for haystacks, the word that Seventh-day Adventists the world over use to refer to what is, essentially, a make-it-yourself taco salad: a foundation of corn chips is topped with beans, cheese, salsa, lettuce, tomatoes, and guacamole or ranch dressing. I couldn't help think now that this might be a kind of peace offering of sorts. My mother, back when she had served as household cook, was often absent or, more accurately, roving on the periphery of conversations and interactions and movie-watching. If it was mealtime, she went to the kitchen and began the requisite preparations. I was doing that now, and that I happened to be readying a staple—if not one of the signature dishes—of Adventist culture was not lost on me. I should say that I know of few meals that are easier to assemble but also more satisfying than haystacks. But it gladdened my heart to know that I had the opportunity to feed my father and aunts and uncles, and to fellowship—a word that I know is not distinctly Adventist, but strikes me as such—with them over a meal that would be both familiar and welcome.

I can no longer remember what we talked about during this meal, only that it began with my Uncle Ted disagreeing with my aunt Melinda about whether or not governments should involve themselves in dictating how their citizens should think or act. I didn't know if anybody else was thinking the thought I was then thinking as we ate, that I had spent a good amount of time with each of the people at this table, but never in this particular configuration. Furthermore, I felt at peace with them. I did not, as I sometimes did, feel the need to mask my awkwardness or pretend that I didn't resent anybody. These were the members of my family. They had loved me my whole life long. And they had my mother. And she them. I had no choice, it seemed, other than to embrace them. To welcome these lovable weirdos into my heart.

Who's to say what choices I might someday make if I were to find myself in my father's situation—if, following a decade in which I presided over my wife's slow-motion demise, I happened to rekindle a long-lost friendship? The phrase "old flame" passed through my mind. The metaphor seemed apt. For as long as I'd known him, my father had loved fires: loved building them, loved lighting them, loved watching them brighten and die. Anyone who knew my father knew this about him. Thinking of my parents' houses often summoned the smell of smoke. The sight of leaping flames. The spray of embers when the poker dug into twinkling chunks of glowing logs, or when newly tossed-on pieces crushed cindery sticks. The slightly lopsided rectangle of extra carpet that lived in front of the hearth and which had been seared in places by live coals the fires of yore had spat out: little black islands of dimpled plastic I often tapped with a finger. No one I knew loved fire more than my father, and no home I could think of had hosted more than our family's, the number of which increased once we moved to the Land and built a house whose living room ceiling was twenty-some feet high, and whose centerpiece was a Rumford fireplace, the design of which had been originally conceived by Count Rumford, an Anglo-American physicist who, thanks to his investigations of heat, developed a fireplace whose shallow, angled sides helped better deflect heat into the room.

During the evenings and on weekends during the winter months, my father took care to build the most extravagant fires, standing back to admire the height of the flames. The fireplace was a stage where something bright and hot and dangerous was contained. You sat before a fire to warm yourself but also to pay homage to its ability to destroy the very home in which it lived. Fire-destroyed homes had always lived a life in my imagination. In one of my earliest memories, I stood at a window I was barely tall enough to peer out of to observe the rarest of sights: the town's fire trucks passing through the cove where we lived. Blinking lights cast shuddering red lights against the trees as they passed the end of the driveway of our old house, to begin their ascent to the top of the mountain, upon which, my father would soon learn, a house had caught fire. Over the years we would pay visits to the charred remains by climbing—and sometimes crawling—through the steep wooded slope behind our house, winding upwards until we reached the road that led to the concrete platform where it had been built. There, we always marveled at the devastation—blackened chunks of wood, a few scorched columns, a murky green swimming pool where dead branches and beer cans bobbed. And we admired the view—the lights of our little town glowing benevolently in the valley below.

Fires required fuel. The main thing was wood. And you had to work to get it. Truck loads of kindling from a nearby lumberyard, logs delivered by patients that sometimes arrived as literal tree trunks, thirty-foot-long behemoths that dad cut into pieces with his Husqvarna, the churning blade spewing fountains of sawdust into the air. He'd roll freshly cut chunks toward a gas-powered wood splitter, position the logs on the machine's metal platform, and yank a joystick-like knob, thereby activating the necessary hydraulics required to thrust the blade through the wood, repeating the process to shave off desired stick sizes, which were then stacked in a truck bed, transported home, and restacked in the garage, and on back and side porches.

My father's fires burst to life in a blaze, growing brightest in their first few minutes. But they don't spend the majority of their lives in such extraordinary fashions. They slow to a steady crackle, flames lapping, cinders pulsing, logs crumbling, scattering into coals below, cooling to ash. And, after the room has gone dark, you can take the little shovel that hangs on a frame with the little broom and poker and churn through the ashes, uncovering orange embers that had been living unseen at the heart of the fire's remains.

Each fire my father has built has lived a unique life—in the living room hearth and in the kitchen's wood stove. Beautiful, lively, warm, light-producing. It made sense to imagine that the fading away of my mother's life was not unlike watching one of my father's fires go out. He'd used up every available resource to maintain her brightness. He'd fed her life's fire every log he could find. After the last stick, he'd had no choice but to watch her life slowly drain, the room cooling and growing dark as it died.

He could have remained in that room. Could've left the hearth cold. Instead, with the help of an old flame, he built a new fire.

On December 21, 2020, the FDA posted translations of its Pfizer-BioNTech COVID-19 vaccine fact sheet in a number of languages, including Arabic, Burmese, Cherokee, Chinese, Chuukese, German, Haitian Creole, Hindi, Hmong, Korean, Mam, Polish, Portuguese, Russian, Spanish, Somali, Tagalog, Vietnamese, and Yiddish. The U. S. Congress approved $900 billion in stimulus funds. This year, the 21st of December marked not only the winter solstice but also, for the first time in twenty years, a great conjunction. Jupiter and Saturn were aligned. According to Black Twitter, this occurrence was granting people superpowers. According to my own horoscope, instead of wringing my hands, I should "treat the process like an adventure." If so, I might find treasure around the corner.

One year before, on the longest night of the year, I'd taken that walk to the golf course hill, and called my father, who'd told me, for the very first time, about the flashing lights in his woods. And now, I thought, exactly one year later, maybe I should embark upon a walk, post-sunset. Head back to the golf course. *Exactly one year later,* I thought, *to the day.* That felt right. A circle. Or maybe the actual date didn't matter. It didn't really have to be the longest night of the year. It might actually be, say, mid-to-late November. Close enough. The point was that I would need to take a walk to the golf course, during a time of darkness. And that time was now. Had been, for weeks: Ever since we turned the clocks back an hour, for which I'd been weirdly grateful that year, the suddenness of which seemed more surreal than in years past. The way the days came so abruptly to an end—it seemed somehow stranger. More pronounced. But also, somehow, more enjoyable?

A few days before, my student Elia had messaged to say, *I'm seriously enjoying the descent into the darkness this year. It's been winter in my heart for like 4 months.*

Winter in my heart, I'd thought.

A beautiful phrase. One that, I was sure, during these times, could describe so many hearts.

On the night I decided to walk to the golf course, I'd watched *My Octopus Teacher*, a documentary that had centered on a middle-aged filmmaker, frustrated with his lack of inspiration, and how he'd started diving into a kelp forest off the coast of South Africa, without a wetsuit, because he wanted nothing to come between him and the environment he was exploring.

During one of these dives, the director finds a pile of shells that suddenly explodes, revealing itself to be an octopus in disguise. The director follows the octopus to her den, which he continues to pay daily visits. I'd sent an invitation to Kelly, who was upstairs watching her own show, and had elected not to watch the octopus movie, because as a rule she never watched movies about animals, because in every movie about animals—especially ones that featured *beloved* animals—they always died, every time; it was as if as soon as a director decided to film an animal that the narrative arc had been automatically decided, and as soon as the director thought, *I'm going to film a movie about this animal*, the animal's fate was sealed: that animal, in other words, would be finished. The directors might as well have said to themselves, *I'm going to slowly kill this animal*, which, in turn, if you have the kind of tenderhearted empathy that Kelly has for all creatures great and small, then watching the slow and steady demise of an animal—whether beloved or not—was nothing more than an exercise in excruciation.

After finishing the film, I texted Kelly to tell her that she'd made the right choice. Of course, she'd already known. Furthermore, she was already sad, as she couldn't stop thinking about the couple we had known—acquaintances, really, that we saw once or twice a year at another mutual friends' house whenever they threw parties—from the Department of Modern and Classical Languages and Literatures, who, after trying for a decade to have a baby, had gotten pregnant but then the wife had given birth to a baby—a boy—and this baby had died. Nobody we knew, except for, presumably, the parents of the child, had known why or how or what had happened except for that single, devastating fact: their baby had died. Though there was literally nothing that I could think of that was sadder than that—Kelly and I had talked about it or, rather, Kelly had talked about it, imagining what it would be like to return home and walk into the nursery that they'd probably decorated with gleeful anticipation— here I was, crying my eyes out because of an octopus who had died. But I wasn't really crying about the octopus, either, which, in the end, the director had learned, had become a mother and produced a baby.

I was crying about my mom.

I didn't try, as I walked out the basement door and cut like I often did through my neighbor's backyard, and then across the street and through a vacant lot and onto the asphalt path that ran behind the new McMansions that had been erected and quickly purchased on the street that was parallel to the one where I lived, to sneak peeks inside the homes. Instead, I wobbled along, eyes brimming with tears, while a drone- like song from a Spotify playlist I'd titled, simply, "ambient," washed through my AirPods and into my ears.

It hadn't been that great a week. I hadn't written anything. Hadn't really tried. I'd spent too much time reading articles about POTUS refusing to leave office and the president's supporters rallying in protest of an election that'd been veri- fied by officials as the most secure ever, and zooming in on maps of the United States that attempted to represent, in red, the extent of the surging virus, and reading about the 27 percent of Americans who were hesitant about the developing vaccine, which my own sister had just received, and hearting movies about mac and cheese recipes.

Now, I was leaving the neighborhood where giant houses had been docked like great ships, and where floodlamps bathed the still-green grass of their immaculate, professionally manicured lawns, to enter the much darker and lightless realm of the Blacksburg municipal golf course.

It was dark in the dark. The sky was clouded. I could barely see to see. At the top of the hill, it was—as usual—windy. I could barely make out the undulating limbs of pine trees that lived on the ridge top. Down below, the lights of Blacksburg glowed: little blurs blushing in the murk. A single red light in the distance blinked. I wondered if it belonged to the coal plant. Nobody else was out. *It's just me*, I thought, and then I said it aloud. "It's just me." But it wasn't. Everyone I'd ever known, I realized, was with me. All those people lived a life inside me, the exact place they'd always lived. It didn't matter if they were dead or alive. They were there and I carried them wherever I went. Including my mother, which seemed appropriate: I'd first come to life inside her body, and she'd carried me, having no idea what I might look like or who I would become. She'd pledged, at the moment of my existence, to love and care for me for her entire life, to put my every need and in many cases wants above her own, to live a life of selflessness and devotion to her husband and children and extended family and friends, never complaining or getting down in the dumps or questioning any part of the moral code by which she lived, the latter of which I greatly resented, perhaps because I myself was so easily agitated and dissatisfied and unable to accept—with the ease with which she had—the beliefs she'd inherited. I could hear her saying, as she always had whenever I complained about her infinitely joyful disposition, *Would you rather have a mean Mama?* As if having a mean mother had been the only alternative to having a joyful one—that you could either have a nice mama or a mean one, a conceit that now struck me as absurdly comical. It hardly seemed right to think of my mother as "gone," because though I could no longer find her physical body in the world, neither could I stop sensing her spirit everywhere I went: I felt as if I had now become pregnant with my mother's presence, but that wasn't quite right because I hoped this new state wasn't as temporary as pregnancy was, and this feeling wasn't a reversal of roles but more like a return. I'd spent so much time worrying about not being able to go home but just as I'd begun life inside her, now I'd returned to a world where my mother was everywhere around me. I could access her spirit anywhere. I could ask her what she thought of Jolene and she'd say, "Is Jolene making your dad happy?" and I'd say, "I think so," and she'd say "Well then be happy for him!" And if I said I was upset because Jolene had taken down all the photographs on the refrigerator—my dad, wearing a light green coat and a CAT hat, holding up a baby wild hog one of our dogs had killed; my grandmother in a picture celebrating her 100th birthday; me in my Superman Underoos, t-shirt and a Kodak camera around my neck, straddling my first bicycle; my grandfather and father sitting beside a campfire; Dad balancing my standing niece, as a baby, in one hand above his head; my grandfather sitting in a chair in his kitchen, with one leg steadying himself on the ledge of an open window, through which he was pointing a rifle, presumably to school a squirrel—I could hear mom's voice saying, "Did Jolene throw the photos away?" And I could say, "No," and "she sent them to me," Mom would say, "Well good!" I complained that it'd been two weeks since Dad had called, I imagined she'd say, "When was the last time *you* called him?" and I'd say, "I don't know" and she'd say, "Then what are you waiting for?!" and then I'd say, "You're right, I don't know," except I did, in fact, know: I hadn't wanted to get into an argument with him about the video he'd sent to my sister about the quack doctor spouting nonsense about the virus or how he'd said that he didn't believe COVID was "that bad" or that he only wore a mask at the office to make other people comfortable. I knew what my mother would say about all this, too, she wouldn't preach or defend him or try to argue me out of my feelings, she'd simply tell me to talk to him, don't treat him like a stranger, reminding me that he was my father and that he loved me and would do anything for me, to which I'd respond, "Except pick up the phone and call his only son," to which she'd say, "Are your fingers broken?" and then she'd laugh as if what she'd just said was the most hilarious thing ever. That too was a sound I could dial up whenever I wanted, and even when I didn't; as long as I'd lived, I'd heard my mother's laughter playing in my head; I supposed I would carry its song to my grave, the entrance into which I did sometimes acknowledge with no small amount of terror, though I had to admit that I too would live on, at least for a while, in the bodies of those who knew me, and that whoever I left behind might also have occasion, as I did my mother's face in the photographs from which she smiled so beautifully and serenely, to find an image of me that might cause them to stop and acknowledge that I was once *so* alive and how sad it seemed that I had no idea what the future held or how or when I too would expire. And yet, look how happy he had been. Once upon a time.

I didn't say my mother's name. But I thought it. *Mom.* I gazed into the darkest part of the fairway. *Mommy.* It was stupid to imagine I might see a flashing light out there, so far from the home where she lived and died, but I couldn't help but wonder.

Mama.

"Open your eyeballs cry-balls," I heard her say, like she used to, when something I was looking for was right in front of me.

So I did.

And so I do.

I keep them open.

And so, I see her wherever I go.

XII. EPILOGUE

Not long after I'd completed an initial draft of this narrative, in December of 2020, my father woke up in the middle of the night. He looked out his window. For the first time in over nine months, he saw something. A flash. In the distance. And then another. And another. The lights were back. Blinking all over. He woke Jolene. She could see them too. And she did. They saw them the next night, and the next.

Creepy, Jolene said, via text.

Beautiful, I replied.

What did Dad think? I didn't ask him. I didn't really need to. Their presence no longer seemed to bother him.

A few nights passed.

Have you seen them again? I asked.

Dad said no. He'd been going to bed early. And kept forgetting to look.

But he promised to do better. To put on his glasses when he woke up in the middle of the night. And look around. Keep his eyes open a while.

If he saw anything, he promised, I would be the first to know.

ACKNOWLEDGEMENTS

Thank you to my mother and father for loving me unconditionally and showing me what it means to live selflessly
and abundantly. Thank you also to Kelly and Elijah for their
undying love and support. Thank you to my sister, Carrie, for
always listening, and her husband, Jesse, for always making
me laugh. Thank you to my agent, Nat Jacks, at Inkwell
Management, for always believing in me and supporting
me. Thank you to Evan Lavender-Smith ("Big Evan") for his
relentless and thorough feedback; without his help and edits
this book would have failed to finally find its form. Thank
you to Meg Reid and Katherine Webb-Hehn at Hub City
for their incredible edits, suggestions, and for shepherding
this book through a thorough and robust revision process.
Thank you to Lee Klein for reading this book, predicting
that it would find a home, and generating a very good title
I did not use. Thank you to Evan Massey ("Lil Evan") for
bearing witness with me and showing me how to be a better
artist. Thank you to Joe Truscello, whose insights about this
book and how it could improve made it better. Thank you to
Jenny Boully and Carmen Giménez for their generous reading of this book and subsequent encouragement. Thank you

to Charles "Fritz" Gritzner for writing *North Carolina Ghost Lights and Legends* and indulging my inquiries. Thank you to Aunt Mary Jane for being, ever since I can remember, a stalwart cheerleader of my life and work and for introducing me, so long ago, to "capital L" literature. Thank you to Luisa Kolker for taking me seriously. Thank you to Mimi Lambert for making me laugh and think twice. Thank you to Scott West for always being such a patient and understanding listener. Thank you to Elia Chaves, Jack Furth, and Chera Longfritz for the conversations. Thank you to Kira Homsher and Shannon Sullivan for reading early versions of this and saying they loved it. Thank you to Brooke Boutwell and Alexis "Lexi" Wiley for writing such incredible sentences and allowing them to live in this book. Thank you to Sy Safransky, who published a small part of this book—the one where my grandmother asks me if I'll smother her with a pillow if she loses her mind—in *The Sun*. Thank you to *Another Chicago Magazine*, who published a small part of this as "Dispatch from a Pandemic." Thank you to Felix and Robert Hooper for going to a VT basketball game the night I first heard about the lights. Thank you to the girls at the office. Thank you to Judy Powell for her love and friendship. Thank you to Jolene for showing up right when Dad needed someone. And thank you to the lights, for greeting me with benevolence and for living a life in my head long after they'd gone out for good.

ABOUT THE AUTHOR

Matthew Vollmer is the author of two short story collections—*Future Missionaries of America* and *Gateway to Paradise*—
as well as three collections of essays—*inscriptions for headstones*,
Permanent Exhibit, and *This World Is Not Your Home*. He was
the editor of *A Book of Uncommon Prayer*, which collects invo-
cations from over sixty acclaimed and emerging authors,
and served as co-editor of *Fakes: An Anthology of Pseudo-
Interviews, Faux-Lectures, Quasi Letters, "Found" Texts, and Other
Fraudulent Artifacts*. His work has appeared in venues such
as the *Paris Review*, *Glimmer Train*, *Ploughshares*, *Tin House*,
Oxford American, the *Sun*, the *Pushcart Prize* anthology, and
Best American Essays. He is Professor of English at Virginia
Tech.

PUBLISHING
New & Extraordinary
VOICES FROM THE
AMERICAN SOUTH

FOUNDED IN SPARTANBURG, South Carolina in 1995, Hub City Press has emerged as the South's premier independent literary press. Hub City is interested in books with a strong sense of place and is committed to finding and spotlighting extraordinary new and unsung writers from the American South. Our curated list champions diverse authors and books that don't fit into the commercial or academic publishing landscape.

HUB CITY PRESS gratefully acknowledges support from the National Endowment for the Arts, the Amazon Literary Partnership, South Arts, and the South Carolina Arts Commission.